FOLK STYLE AUTOHARP

An Instruction Method for Playing the Autoharp and Accompanying Folk Songs

BY HARRY TAUSSIG

OAK PUBLICATIONS, NEW YORK

Book design by Jean Hammons

1st Printing-	September 1967
2nd Printing-	July 1968
3rd Printing-	October 1969
4th Printing-	May 1970

©1967 Oak Publications
A Division of Embassy Music Corp.,
33 West 60th St., New York 10023

SBN # 8256-0021-9

Library of Congress Catalogue Card No. 67-27260

Printed in the United States of America

To Sioux

Photographs

Page

8   HARRY A. TAUSSIG, Photo by Sioux Taussig
25   SYLVIA, Photo by David Gahr
26   MEMBERS OF E.V. STONEMAN FAMILY,
        Courtesy of FOLKWAYS RECORDS
33   KILBY SNOW, Photo by Mike Seeger,
        Courtesy of FOLKWAYS RECORDS
36   KILBY AND JIM SNOW, Photo by Mike Seeger,
        Courtesy of FOLKWAYS RECORDS
37   KILBY AND JIM SNOW, Photo by Mike Seeger,
        Courtesy of FOLKWAYS RECORDS
38   JIM AND KILBY SNOW, Photo by Mike Seeger,
        Courtesy of FOLKWAYS RECORDS
39   NERIAH AND KENNETH BENFIELD, Photo by Mike Seeger,
        Courtesy of FOLKWAYS RECORDS
41   NERIAH AND KENNETH BENFIELD, Photo by Mike Seeger,
        Courtesy of FOLKWAYS RECORDS
42   BILL KEITH, Photo by David Gahr
44   KILBY SNOW, Photo by David Gahr
45   PEGGY SEEGER, Photo by David Gahr
52   Photo by David Gahr
55   ERNEST V. STONEMAN, Photo by Mike Seeger,
        Courtesy of FOLKWAYS RECORDS
59   MIKE SEEGER, Photo by Raeburn Flerlage
72   MAYBELLE CARTER, Photo by Herb Peck, Jr.
77   MAYBELLE CARTER, Photo by David Gahr
79   Photo by David Gahr

Contents

Page

9 INTRODUCTION
10 The Autoharp: Its Origin and Development from a
Popular to a Folk Instrument, by A. Doyle Moore

21 BEGINNING ACCOMPANIMENTS
(24) Go Tell Aunt Rhody
(25) Red River Valley
(26) Lonesome Valley

27 READING MELODIES
(29) Wildwood Flower
(30) Red River Valley
(31) Lonesome Valley
(32) Banks of the Ohio
(33) Hard Ain't It Hard

34 MELODY PICKING ON AUTOHARP
(35) Banks of the Ohio
(36) Hard Ain't It Hard
(37) Red River Valley
(38) Lonesome Valley
(39) Wildwood Flower
(40) Wagoner's Lad - 3/4 Time

41 MORE CHORDS AND KEYS
(42) Wildwood Flower
(43) Bury Me Beneath The Willow - G
(44) Wildwood Flower - F
(45) I Never Will Marry - 3/4 Time
(46) Down In The Willow Garden - 3/4 Time, F
(48) Engine 143 - 3/4 Time
(49) Railroad Bill
(50) John Hardy

51 OFF-BEATS AND SYNCOPATION
(53) Railroad Bill
(54) Golden Vanity
(56) Keep On The Sunny Side
(57) Rosewood Casket - G
(58) The Storms Are On The Ocean - 3/4 Time, F
(60) Forsaken Love - 3/4 Time, F
(61) Black Jack David - F

62 DEVELOPMENT OF INSTRUMENTAL SOLOS
(62) Little Moses - 3/4 Time
(64) Railroad Bill
(65) Man of Constant Sorrow

66 WORKING FROM SONG BOOKS
(66) Pack Up Your Sorrows
(68) Pack Up Your Sorrows
(69) Pack Up Your Sorrows
(70) Pack Up Your Sorrows
(71) Pack Up Your Sorrows

72 SOME FANCY SOLOS
(73) White Cockade
(74) Grandfather's Clock
(75) Pretty Peggy-O
(76) Bully of The Town

78 EXPERIMENTAL AUTOHARP
(78) Little Maggie

80 Selected Discography and Bibliography

Harry A. Taussig has been interested in traditional and contemporary folk instrumental styles on guitar, banjo and autoharp for the past seven years. He has authored, Instrumental Techniques of American Folk Guitar, an instruction book on traditional guitar styles including Carter Picking and Fingerpicking. He has been writing instruction articles for Sing Out! magazine for the past year. He has recorded for Talisman and Takoma recording companies. He is currently teaching music in Los Angeles and working on his Doctoral degree in Biophysics at UCLA.

Introduction

It has been the author's attempt to present, in a concise form, an introduction to the country style of playing the Autoharp. The styles presented have been kept as general as possible so the student can apply the techniques to any specific artist he wishes to study. Once the student has mastered the material in this book, he will have no difficulty in studying various traditional artists, or, on the other hand, supplementing his repertoire by his own arrangements and compositions.

The major difficulty in preparing a book such as this is to invent a notation that is easier to read than the autoharp is to play. I have retained the musical notation because it gives the "shape" of the melody. In addition, music reading skill will be necessary for working from other printed sources. The music is supplemented by simple notation which indicates how the autoharp is to be played. I would like to thank Mr. Mayne Smith for fruitful discussions in regard to the notation used in this book.

FROM "NEW YORK FOLKLORE QUARTERLY", VOLUME 19, NUMBER 4 (DECEMBER, 1963):

✦✦✦✦✦✦✦✦✦✦✦✦✦

THE AUTOHARP: ITS ORIGIN AND DEVELOPMENT FROM A POPULAR TO A FOLK INSTRUMENT

A. DOYLE MOORE

"BE IT known that I, Charles F. Zimmermann . . . have invented certain new and useful Improvements in Harps. . . . A harp so provided has the size of a zither, and which I term an 'autoharp,' and the manner in which the instrument is played is entirely new." [1] These words were contained in the inventor's patent application, (257,808) filed on December 10, 1881. He had coined the new instrument's name while perfecting his models and drawings. Although Zimmermann's autoharp and its successors have been manufactured continuously for nearly 80 years and have been much used by folk musicians in the Southern Highlands for half a century, it has not been described, historically or stylistically, in academic journals. My personal curiosity as to the autoharp's technical development and folk role came after I learned to play. The paucity of recent literature on the instrument led me to its present site of production, Jersey City, New Jersey, and from there back by stages to the home of its gifted creator.

Charles Zimmermann had worked at many jobs in the 48 years before he came to Philadelphia from Germany in 1865. Here he joined his brother in the musical instrument sales and repair

✦✦✦✦✦✦✦✦✦✦✦✦✦✦✦✦✦✦✦✦✦✦✦✦✦✦✦✦✦✦✦✦✦✦✦✦

business and here he became a United States citizen. All his jobs in the old country had been in the music field where he had successfully improved the mechanical function of the accordion. Zimmermann's dedication to the accordion, he was to write in later years,[2] followed the acclamation accorded him and his dance music by Danzig newspapers. He now determined to build a bigger instrument. Working with the mechanical production of notes and chords gave Zimmermann an insight into music that led him to establish a number system of notation. He vowed that music was of divine origin, but its divinity could not reach out to the notation system regularly used.

The Zimmermann note system was described by its inventor in 1871 as "representing the dawn of a new era in written music by means of figures, contrasting in a great measure with the millenium of darkest night which reigns, while the custom of writing music in that tedious and fanciful manner flourished."[3] The dawn could not be brought to light and after several years of struggle in revising his system three times and in making fruitless trips abroad, Zimmermann decided to produce an instrument that could be played only by understanding his unwelcome system of figure notation. He was to write of his greatest work:

> However, since I recognized more and more how difficult it would be to introduce such a new (tone numbering) system, I completely took my thoughts off the union accordion to a string instrument with bars which were supposed to regulate the chords in all keys by suppressing the sound of all other strings. After two years of continuous experiments, I now have brought this instrument, the autoharp, to its utmost perfection. I believe it is the best work which a human being so far has achieved on earth. It is not only an agreeable instrument which can be learned most easily, but it is also a mechanical "self teacher" in sound and abbreviated notation of all possible harmonies of the new tone-number system. . . .[4]

First production of the autoharp started in 1885 at Zimmermann's plant workshop on Second Street, in Philadelphia. During the first three years over 50,000 instruments were sold. Its fascination, however, was that of a toy rather than a serious musical contribution, and the new instrument continued for some time as a novelty in the gadget-happy Victorian period.[5] A remnant of Zimmermann's uninspired success is found in an entry in the first *Sears-Roebuck Catalog*, 1894: "A practical and ingenious musical novelty—Consists of a zither with an attachment for producing chords. . . ."[6]

In the catalogs of the following 11 years, autoharp advertising moved from a tiny illustration to a full three-quarter page with five illustrated models and with an accolade to its well-deserved popularity as a musical instrument. During this period other mechanical chord producing instruments — the apolloharp and mellowharp — were introduced. After a short two-season existence (at the same price), they both were dropped from the catalog while the autoharp producer continued to increase its model numbers and lower its prices.

Style No. 1. $4.00

Style No. 1 has 21 strings and 3 bars, producing the three chords of the key of C, C and F Major, and G Seventh. Thumb pick, brass pick, music rack, tuning key and instruction book containing 11 pieces of music. Nicely packed.

Style No. 6. $25.00

Style No. 6 has 32 strings, 6 bars and 10 metal shifters, producing 16 chords. 400 pieces of music (our complete catalogue) may be played on this style. Inlaid edges, handsome finish. Nicely packed. Very complete furnishings.

Style No. 4. $15.00

Style No. 4 has 7 strings and 5 bars, with 6 metal shifters, producing 11 chords. Thumb pick, brass pick, music rack, tuning key and instruction book containing 24 pieces of music. Nicely packed.

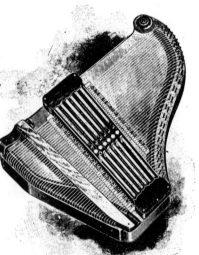

Style "Concert Harp." $150.00

Style "Concert Harp" has 54 strings. This instrument produces 72 chords, comprising all the Major, Minor, Seventh and Diminished Seventh chords of every key, as well as a number of compound chords. Tone quality: rich, full, sympathetic. For solo and orchestral work. Finish and equipment commensurate with price. The Perfect Autoharp.

An 1895 advertisement for four popular models of autoharps. A 1963 manufacturer sells a 12-chord standard model for $34.95 and a "15-chord Deluxe Golden Autoharp" for $39.95.

At the same time, other economic developments were taking place that would affect the history of the autoharp. As a result of the lowering of restrictions on imports with the new tariffs of the Cleveland Administration, many businesses suffered an economic slump. One such business was that of Alfred Dolge, an important manufacturer of piano parts. In an effort to combat his losses, he looked about for a new product that could be manufactured at his Dolgeville, New York, plant. Dolge had selected this location on Canada Creek for its source of pure water (important in the manufacture of top grade felts) and for the native hardwoods so important in making piano sounding boards.[7] He wanted to be the best manufacturer of every part of the piano. With the addition of a wire factory, Dolge controlled everything but the African elephant, his source of ivory. He saw in the Zimmermann instrument a new use for his materials and set about organizing the C. F. Zimmermann Autoharp Company.

On December 23, 1892, Alfred Dolge purchased the controlling stock in the Company, and by January 13, 1893, he had moved the entire manufacturing plant from Philadelphia to its new location in the Adirondack foothills. His Dolgeville work force was augmented by Zimmermann's Philadelphia mechanics. It is a commentary on Dolge's business acumen that this entire transition took place within a period of three weeks. In the first week of work in the new location, 3,000 autoharps were produced.[8]

As an acknowledged authority on musical instruments[9] and a successful and wealthy business man, Alfred Dolge surrounded himself with able newspaper writers, advertising men and promoters as well as leading figures in the music world. In the span of five years, the combined force had established the autoharp as "America's Favorite Instrument," a slogan gracefully embellished with a golden eagle holding the instrument. A minor classical composer, Scharwenka, wrote a minuet for the autoharp, and the much improved concert model was featured in Gilmore's Band under the direction of Victor Herbert. Touring the country with the band, in the years from 1895 through 1897, Aldis Gery established a reputation as the world's greatest autoharp performer.[10]

The autoharp increased in popularity as vast sums were spent on advertising. Sales mounted with such rapidity that the factory was taxed to its utmost and had to be enlarged. The business during this time was under the management of Rudolf Dolge, Alfred's eldest son. The rage for the autoharp spread. Every jobber and dealer in musical merchandise wanted it. An assured fortune seemed in sight until Mr. Dolge, or some newly appointed manager, conceived a scheme having disastrous results. This new plan forced dealers, by means of an iron-clad agreement, to do business on a ten percent margin and to sell at certain figures specified in the contract. The result was a general revolt, and hundreds of dealers, some of the largest in the country, refused to handle the autoharp at any price. The situation was aggravated by the plant manager who stated in an interview that Dolge had no use for the dealer and intended to sell directly to the public.[11]

During this same period, an effort was made to establish contact in the previously unexploited South by entering an elaborate exhibit in the Cotton States International Exposition, at Atlanta, in 1895. The hiring of door-to-door teacher-salesmen along with the market supplied by Sears-Roebuck and Montgomery Ward enabled Alfred Dolge to salvage some of his business, but it prospered only briefly. Because of personal involvements, the amassed Dolge businesses failed, and the golden age of autoharp production began a decline.

Autoharp advertising in popular magazines during this "hard-time" era consisted of much smaller and less effective displays at a time when they were competing with ads for the newly-perfected phonograph.[12] According to one commentator, "It became easier to wind the crank of a talking machine than to pick the strings of the autoharp."[13] Nevertheless, by the year 1897 Alfred Dolge and Son had produced for Americans close to a half million autoharps at the rate of 3,000 a week many of which, in the future, would be relegated to attics, trash heaps and second-hand stores.

The company tried to maintain its momentum after 1897, but without the guidance and promotional abilities of Alfred Dolge, it was forced to halt production. At the time the factories closed, thousands of autoharps, complete except for stringing, were burned.[14]

The competitive Phonoharp Company's product had never shared the popularity of the autoharp, but about 1910 it obtained the patents and rights to manufacture autoharps. The less-desirable phonoharp was dropped, and the Boston firm now put its full efforts into producing the new instrument. None of the models was modified, although the concert grand and several of the more expensive items were dropped while the company started tediously to reestablish the autoharp as a parlor instrument. With only a modest catalog and house-to-house salesmen, Phonoharp succeeded because the appeal for the autoharp had moved from the privacy of the parlor to recreational gatherings, hospital wards and classrooms. It became the portable "mountain piano" of itinerant preachers. It was used to entertain hospital patients and it also became a tool in physical therapy. As many Red Cross workers were school teachers, the instrument found its way into grade school classes.

In 1926, the Phonoharp Company merged with Oscar Schmidt International, Incorporated, of Jersey City. The merged firms now employ a force of 20 to 30 men and produce 400 instruments a week, mainly as school harmony teaching aids.[15] Its school popularity was demonstrated in 1952 in the city of its invention when 24 autoharps were played by children as a part of a program of the Music Educators National Conference.[16] This sight would have pleased Charles Zimmermann although the youngsters were playing from manuscripts covered with notes—tools with which the "godly qualities of music were suppressed for almost 1000 years by the Jesuits and Pharisees because of the notation." [17]

The Schmidt-produced instrument of today looks, responds, and sounds no different from the oldest Zimmermann model on view at the museum of the Washington State Historical Society, in Tacoma. The physical structure has never effectively changed, yet, as has been mentioned, the autoharp has been used for four separate purposes: first, it served as a device to promote a note system; second, as a toy or novelty; third, as a popular parlor and concert instrument; and fourth, as a music education aid. This pattern of use indicates that the instrument can be easily adapted to various roles by the performer, thereby helping to explain its transformation to a folk instrument.

It is doubtful that there were phonograph recordings of performances on the autoharp before 1900 because the well-expressed purpose of the manufacturer was to sell the instrument and not the sound or song. An early printed house organ from Alfred Dolge and Son shows in the masthead a cartoon depicting the burning of a phonograph with caricatures of company officials stopping the pumping of water and fanning the blaze instead.[18] Contemporary accounts of performances and concerts provide no basis for duplicating the sound or judging the effect of playing in the popular manner of the late 1890's.

An interview (July 15, 1962) with Mr. E. Stone, a 92-year old resident of Dolgeville, gave me my first and only idea of the autoharp's sound in the days before recordings. Stone was a personal friend of Robin Tracy, one of the last teacher-salesmen for the Dolgeville plant. Stone enabled me to appreciate the manner in which the instrument was popularly played. It could best be described as "an endless succession of arpeggios made by graceful swoops across the strings."[19] Truly, the sound was as haunting as an echo.[20] It is conceivable that the autoharp as played in its formative years could have become the harp of David, but such divinity would have relied strongly on the elaborately prepared music sheets of Zimmermann and the teaching of his disciple, Tracy.

Seemingly, Zimmermann, Dolge, Gery, Tracy, and their peers accepted the heavenly sounds of the autoharp without considering the possibility of alternative modes. Fortunately, a number of gifted folk performers operating outside the bounds of composed music, both classical and popular, took up the instrument. The first and most important of such autoharpists of whom knowledge is available is Ernest V. "Pop" Stoneman, from southwestern Virginia, an area steeped in traditional folksong.[21]

Stoneman was born in Carroll County, Virginia, the same year that Alfred Dolge bought and moved the Philadelphia autoharp factory to its upper Mohawk Valley location. As a boy, Ernest had heard his Grandmother Bowers play on her autoharp the hymn "Nearer My God to Thee." The lad was impressed by the sweetness of the instrument and wanted to master it. Already proficient on the harmonica, it was no trouble to pick melodies and strum the easy chords on the new instrument. At the age of eight, "Pop" recalls playing "Old Molly Hare" on an autoharp he acquired by trading. Unhampered and unaware of the vast storehouse of music sheets and instruction books, young Ernest was left entirely to himself to master the wondrous workings of the autoharp.

Devising a complex wire clip for the right hand index finger, he was able to flip as well as drag his finger across the strings at the bottom of the instrument. With a sort of pinching motion, melody notes could be accurately sounded. With dexterity in depressing the appropriate chord bars, fast songs were produced—songs that would have taxed Zimmermann's number note system no end. "Pop's" uncles and friends in the community had autoharps, but were not as skilled as Stoneman. These relatives and neighbors eventually ceased to play, stating that the instruments were too hard to tune, that they fell apart, and that they were difficult to repair. "Pop" was not daunted by such problems. He continued to buy new instruments, owning many during the span of his playing years, tuning them and repairing them as best he could. A good mechanic and inventor, "Pop" built a large autoharp out of a discarded piano, but it proved too cumbersome for use.

Not only was Stoneman inventive, but he was curious and imaginative as well. When he heard the newly-made recordings of Henry Whitter, also from Carroll County, "Pop" felt he could play more expertly the native music. In New York City, on September 1, 1924, he made for Okeh the first recording of autoharp music with "The Face that Never Returned" and "The Sinking of the Titantic" (40288). At this pioneer session, using the carrying case as a sounding box, he played his instrument into the acoustical recording horn. Ralph Peer, Okeh's recording director, was delighted with the sound of the autoharp and told Stoneman he had "found his niche." His previous singing and playing had been confined to home, church, social dances, or outings; now "Pop" could be heard by many more people than could be gathered together for a picnic. A photograph in the May, 1925, *Okeh Catalog* shows Stoneman in the attitude of playing with a harmonica around his neck and the autoharp on top of its box in his lap. The discs and many additional instruments displayed at his side give us, today, a graphic view of the exciting advertising in the musical idiom soon to be termed "hillbilly."

A comprehensive listing of autoharp recordings and performers has not yet been compiled. From the time of Stoneman's first record (1924) until World War II, the following folk performers made one or more records using the instrument: Carson Brothers and Smith, Will Abernathy with Tom Ashley, Smith Brothers, the Chumbler Family, Lee Brothers Trio, Floyd Ming and his Pep-steppers, Dykes' Magic City Trio and the Carter Family. Of these, the Carter Family — Maybelle, her cousin, Sarah, and Sarah's husband, A. P. Carter — is distinguished as one of the most important influences on American country music.[22] The autoharp that Sarah Carter chorded only acted as a foil to the rythmic melodic lines of Maybelle Carter's guitar. Yet the use of the autoharp was highly significant in the instrumental styling of the nearly 300 songs in their recorded repetoire. Sarah Carter played an eight bar autoharp with 32 strings, a chromatic scale producing the chords C, F, and B flat major; C, G, and A seventh; and D and G minor, giving a range of playing in the keys of C and F major and D minor. When she switched to a guitar, it was to play in the keys of A, D, and G major. Had she owned one of the more complex models, we might never have heard Sarah Carter play guitar. She was proficient with many instruments, but the autoharp was her first choice in ensemble playing.

Maybelle Carter had played with her parent's autoharp as a small girl in Scott County, Virginia, an area similar to Stoneman's Blue Ridge Mountain background. With the help and encouragement of her brothers and sisters, Maybelle became a good banjo picker. Her brother played the guitar and taught her rhythm and style. It is this guitar playing that gives a sustaining quality to music now categorized as "Carter Family songs." Maybelle never played the autoharp with the original Carter Family, but after the trio disbanded in 1943, she developed a unique and now much-copied style of playing the melody.

Maybelle frequently tuned Sarah's autoharp during studio recording sessions, and it is easy to see the development from the single response of a string being tuned to the possibility of producing a melodic line. In this period, Maybelle's method did not differ greatly from Stoneman's. Both excited the strings at the bottom of the instrument.

In 1945, Maybelle and her three daughters — Helen, June and Anita — formed a performing group and toured the country as "Mother Maybelle and the Carter Sisters." Maybelle bought an autoharp for June to play, but it was left to Maybelle to experiment and develop it into a lead instrument. Discovering that sweeter tones could be produced by playing the autoharp's top half where the strings are more flexible and harp-like, Maybelle crossed her hands and played in this new manner. Since much of the playing was done at public performances, it was never certain if a table would be provided for Maybelle's use. But by hoisting the instrument up to her breast, Maybelle freed herself from the need of a table and chair. The instrument was now mobilized so she could move to or away from the microphone. By changing her hand to an up and down movement rather than back and forth, she gave herself a tactile relationship to the strings, so that her "licks" became more like the playing of a guitar and less like the previous scrubbing technique. This added richness and life can readily be heard by comparing Sarah's and Maybelle's method on LP reissues of original Carter Family records with the recent LP offering made by Maybelle. This contrast demonstrates that the instrument is capable of responding to selective movements as well as producing a music born of its own unique features.[23]

Just as other instruments began as melodic imitators either of the human voice or earlier instruments and then evolved their own intricate musical expressions so did the autoharp. A contemporary example of the autoharp's evolution and the development of its instrumental style is found in *Mountain Music Played on the Autoharp* (Folkways FA 2365) by Ernest Stoneman, Kilby Snow and a pair of father and son performers, Neriah and Kenneth Benfield. This disk clearly demonstrates the unique and personal relationship that develops between the player and his instrument.

The four players on this Folkways release were recorded by Mike Seeger. Seeger, also an autoharp performer, has an interest and performing skill so infectious that following each of his concerts (solo or with the New Lost City Ramblers) a new crop of potential and often productive players is born. My own involvement with the instrument came after attending such a concert.

After learning some of the historical background of the auto-harp I turned to the Library of Congress and its Archive of American Folk Music to try to locate autoharp field recordings, only to find that out of 70,000 entries gathered by 130 collectors, not one disc or tape held the sound of the autoharp.[24] Puzzled by this finding I left Washington, and half a day later was talking to Israel Welch, a West Virginia farmer, who was reported by his neighbors to have played an autoharp. Much to my delight, I learned he had played the instrument, as well as the fiddle and guitar, and in the early 1930's had headed a string band composed of his brothers. He states that a Library of Congress collector had recorded the band but Welch never mentioned that he played the autoharp. The collector could never have guessed that the autoharp was a part of Welch's private life at home, where he used it to play hymns and to second his brother's fiddle. I sensed Welch's apology for the handed-down instrument.[25]

The reluctance to use the autoharp in public still exists among some performers. Such players show a self-conscious attempt to hide their feelings for what they consider an ignoble instrument. The autoharp and its music are ridiculed and have been named: idiot zither, push-button music, instant music.

However, not all performers apologize for the autoharp. "Pop" Stoneman, Maybelle Carter, and others see and feel its beauty and have adapted it to a rich body of traditional folk music. The in-ventor, Charles Zimmermann, created the autoharp as a mechani-cal aid in teaching his tone number system. Fortunately, the in-strument fell into the hands of folk performers, not only unac-quainted with his system, but not dependent on any musical nota-tion. They responded to its charm, and by their natural musical abilities, turned the autoharp into an American folk instrument.

------

[1] United States Patent Office, *Specifications and Drawings of Patents,* (Washing-ton, May 1882), 823-825.

[2] On a visit to the Dolgeville Public Library (July 16, 1962) the Librarian, Mrs. Rita Rockwell, made available to me an uncataloged collection of Rudolph Dolge papers. Included was an unpublished autobiographical manuscript in German by C. F. Zimmermann, which has been translated by Gisela Swanson, Urbana, Illinois. A copy of the original, the translation, and other material gathered for this study are deposited in the archives of the John Edwards Memorial Foundation, University of California, Los Angeles. Quotations from the manuscript translation in these notes are referred to as Zimmermann MS.

[3] C. F. Zimmermann, *C. F. Zimmermann's Simplified Harmony Teacher and Short-Hand Writing of Chords,* (Philadelphia), 8. Copies of this booklet, as well as brochures and clippings from the Dolge papers referred to in footnotes 5, 8, 10, 11, 18, and 20, are deposited in the John Edwards Memorial Foundation.

[4] Zimmermann MS, 3.

5 *The Dolgeville Herald,* February 6, 1896, 1.

6 *Sears-Roebuck and Company General Catalog No. 100,* (Chicago, 1894), 250.

7 *Herkimer County Commemorative Brochure,* (Herkimer, New York, 1954), 36.

8 *Little Falls Journal and Courier: Industrial Edition,* (December, 1895), 25.

9 Harvey N. Roehl, *Player Piano Treasury,* (Vestal, New York, 1961), 4. This publication provides a recent account of Dolge's classic history of the piano.

10 *Freund's Musical Weekly,* May 15, 1895.

11 *The Music Trades,* December 21, 1895.

12 Magazines in which the autoharp ads appeared, with 1895 circulation figures: *Century* (175,000), *Scribner's* (132,500), *Cosmopolitan* (200,000), *Munsey's* (300,000), *Ladies' Home Journal* (710,000), *Youth's Companion* (540,000), *Harper's* (175,000), *McClure's* (60,000), *Review of Reviews* (102,000), *Chatauquan* (100,000), *Christian Herald* (120,000), *Golden Rule* (83,500), *Epworth Herald* (97,700).

13 *Little Falls Evening Times,* October 26, 1938.

14 *Ibid.,* February, 1951.

15 Interview with H. G. Finney, Manager, Oscar Schmidt International Inc., Jersey City, January 31, 1962.

16 A firm specializing in school sales of autoharps is National Autoharp Sales Company, P.O. Box 1120, Des Moines, Iowa.

17 Zimmermann MS, 4.

18 *The Autoharp,* January 28, 1893, reproduced in *The Musical Courier,* February 8, 1893.

19 Peter Seeger, "The Autoharp, Played Stoneman Style," *Sing Out,* XI (December, 1961), 16-17.

20 *American Art Journal,* January 5, 1895.

21 Biographical information on Stoneman was gathered in an interview with him at his home in Washington, D. C., January 30, 1962.

22 Archie Green, "The Carter Family's 'Coal Miner's Blues,' " *Southern Folklore Quarterly,* XXV (December, 1961), 226-237.

23 Information on Maybelle Carter's playing style was gathered in an interview with her in Madison, Tennessee, September 9, 1962.

24 Interview with Rae Korson, Head, Archive of Folksong, Library of Congress, Washington, July 20, 1962.

25 Interview with Israel Welch, Burlington, West Virginia, July 21, 1962.

CHAPTER I - BEGINNING ACCOMPANIMENTS

We will begin playing the autoharp by learning to accompany the singing of some common folk songs. We will later develop some of the songs into instrumental solos to be played on the autoharp. For all our work on the autoharp, the right hand will pick the strings and the left hand will operate the chord bars.

There are three ways to hold the autoharp while playing it. The first is flat on the lap (or on a table) with the right hand picking the strings to the <u>right</u> (on the short end) of the chord bars. This is shown in Figure 1.

This is the best way to practice the accompaniments in this chapter and new tunes that you will be learning in the future chapters of this book.

Figure #1

The second way to play the autoharp is for the right hand to play to the <u>left</u> of the chord bars. This achieves better sound, but you cannot always see what the left hand is doing because it involves crossing the hands, as shown in Figure 2.

Figure #2

When you have become familiar with the accompaniment or a solo you can hold the autoharp up against your chest as shown in Figure 3.

Figure #3

In this position you cannot see where either hand is playing, so some familiarity with the autoharp is necessary before this is attempted. It is always best to start learning a song with the A-harp flat on the lap.

We will now discuss in some detail what the right and left hands will be doing. The left hand is used to operate the chords bars. The three chord bars that will be required for the songs in the first few chapters are C, F, and G7 (notice that these are not the C7 and G). The best way to play the three chords required is to use one finger for each chord bar. While playing the autoharp flat on the lap, use the index finger to play the F chord bar, the middle finger to play the G7 chord bar and the ring finger to play the C chord bar. This is shown in Figure 1. By letting the fingers rest lightly on the bars and only depressing the bar as needed, you can play by "touch" and avoid hunting for the bars. Needless to say, you will have to change the fingering slightly when you play with the 'harp in the vertical position. There it is even more important to play by "touch" since you usually can't see where the bars are.

As mentioned above the right hand will be responsible for playing the actual melodies and the accompaniments on the autoharp. For the time being, we will be using only the thumb of the right hand. You will want to wear a thumb pick as shown in Figure 4.

Figure #4

The thumb will play two types of notes in our accompaniments: these will be called the <u>thumb notes</u> and the <u>brush notes</u>. The thumb note consists of a short stroke in the bass portion of the machine. This is illustrated in Figure 5.

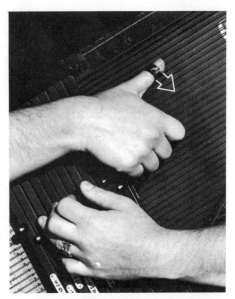

Figure #5

This stroke is about one or two inches long, and, when a chord bar is held down, will sound only two or three strings. The brush stroke starts where the thumb stroke ended! It continues on for about four or five inches from the bass into the middle portion of the A-harp as shown in Figure 6.

Figure #6

The combination the "thumb-brush" will occur very frequently in your autoharp playing so it will be discussed in some detail. This figure consists of a short stroke, a pause, and then the thumb <u>continues</u> across the strings. It is important to start the brush stroke in the same area where the thumb stroke ended and not to "back up" into the bass. The sound that is achieved in this way is very similar to the "Carter style" guitar picking. In this style the bass note (also played by the thumb) is very distinct from the brushed chord that follows. For more on Carter style guitar, see the references in the Bibliography.

Now let's put the whole thing together. Hold down a C chord bar. Count out loud, slowly and evenly,

1, 2, 3, 4; 1, 2, 3, 4; ...

Then, in the same rhythm, play

Thumb, Brush, Thumb, Brush; Thumb, Brush, Thumb, Brush; ... This is the basic accompaniment!

It is often a good idea to move the thumb around a bit when playing the Thumb note. You will find that it sounds better in some places than others. Now try the same thing with the F and G7 chord bars. Take note of the places where the thumb notes sound best for each chord. Also practice changing chord bars while playing the accompaniment. Notice that if you hold down two chord bars at the same time you don't get much of anything and if you play without holding down any chord bars, the roof caves in.

The two types of notes we have learned so far will be indicated in this book in the following way. The thumb note will be indicated by a capital letter T. The brush note will be abbreviated by an arrow pointing upwards.

Below is given the notation to our first song and accompaniment, Go Tell Aunt Rhody. There are four things given in this notation: 1) the words (you should know the melodies of this first song well enough to sing along), 2) the indications for the Thumb notes and the Brush notes (T's and arrows), 3) the particular chord bar required to accompany the melody (given below the words) and 4) for the first few measures the count, 1, 2, 3, 4, etc. is given. This song should be practiced slowly and evenly until confidence is gained in both the right hand accompaniment and the left hand changing the chords bars.

GO TELL AUNT RHODY

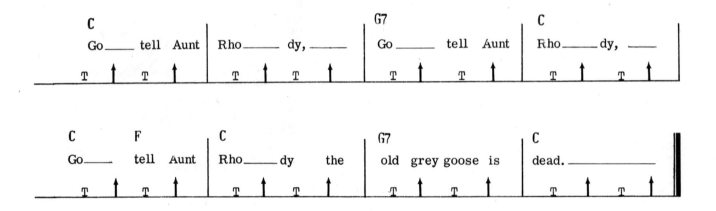

The one she's been savin',
The one she's been savin',
The one she's been savin',
To make her feather bed.

She drownded in the millpond, (3X)
Standing on her head.

The old gander's weepin', (3X)
Because his wife is dead.

The goslin's are mournin', (3X)
Because their mammy's dead.

The best way to learn a skill well is to practice it. The following songs should provide the student with some material to practice the basic accompaniments on. In addition, the student should supplement this with songs he already knows.

Our second song, Red River Valley, starts on count 3, which is a thumb note. This should present no difficulty. Notice that the 1 and 2 beats of that first measure are made up in the last measure of the song. Many tunes in song books are written this way and the student should get used to starting a song on any beat in the measure.

RED RIVER VALLEY

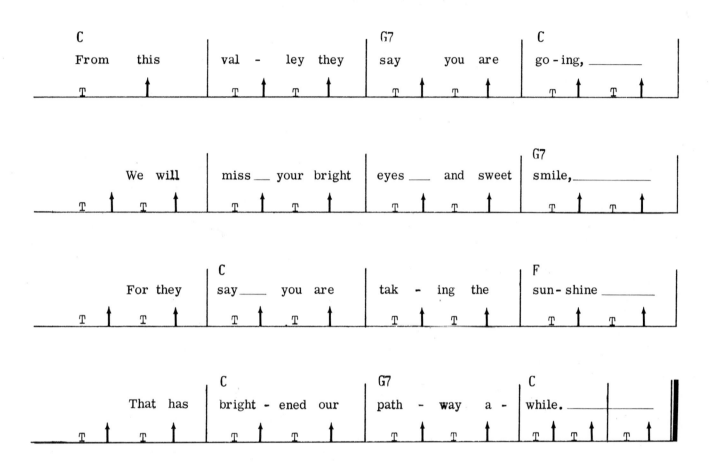

CHORUS:

Come and sit by my side, if you love me,
Do not hasten to bid me adieu,
Just remember the Red River Valley
And the cowboy who loved you so true.

I've been thinking a long time, my darling,
Of the sweet words you never would say,
Now, alas, must my fond hopes all vanish?
For they say you are going away.

Do you think of the valley you're leaving?
Oh, how lonely and how dreary it will be.
Do you think of the kind hearts you're breaking?
And the pain you are causing to me?

They will bury me where you have wandered,
Near the hills where the daffodils grow,
When you're gone from the Red River Valley,
For I can't live without you I know.

The last example in this chapter, Lonesome Valley, starts on the second beat of the measure, this corresponds to a brush note in our basic accompaniment. If this is difficult, try starting the accompaniment on the first beat with a thumb note, and then start singing on the second beat. You can also do this when working out of song books when you find a song that starts on the second beat, or in some other uncomfortable place.

LONESOME VALLEY

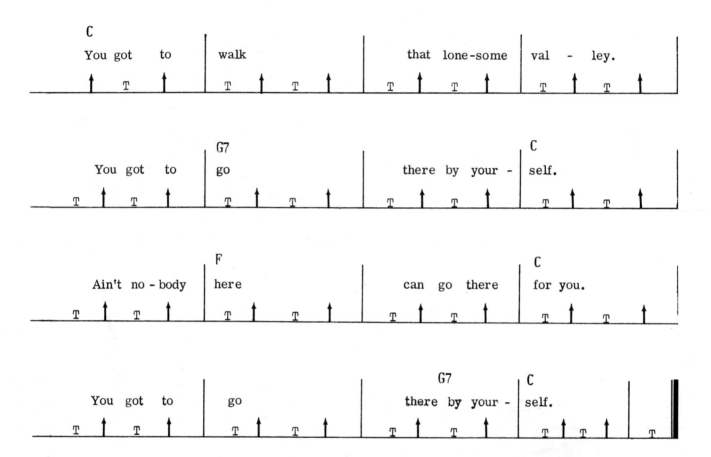

If you cannot preach like Peter,
If you cannot pray like Paul,
You can tell the love of Jesus,
You can say he died for all.

Your mother's got to walk that lonesome valley,
She's got to go there by herself,
Ain't nobody else can go there for her,
She's got to go there by herself.

Your father's got to walk that lonesome
    valley...

Your brother's got to walk that lonesome
    valley...

CHAPTER II - READING MELODIES

Now that we have learned to accompany a song on the autoharp, we will learn to play the melodies for several songs. For picking out melodies on the autoharp we will use the index finger of the right hand. You will have to use a finger pick as shown in Figure 7 (not using a pick tends to get blood on the autoharp). A plastic fingerpick gives a very nice sound.

Figure #7

You will find that metal picks, Figure 8, have a slightly different sound and later you will want to change picks for different songs. Some traditional players use metal thimbles to pick the melody, this gives a very zingy sound. To make the thimbles fit your fingers, try stepping on them (without your finger inside). However, the plastic fingerpicks are best for starting out.

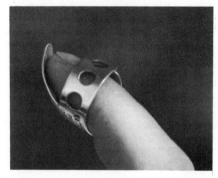

Figure #8

To learn to play melodies out of a song book requires some knowledge of reading music. I strongly recommend that the student who is not familiar or not comfortable with standard music notation to look at the accompanying table. The ten minutes spent reading and studying it will be well worth while. In this chart are given all the rules necessary to read all the music in this book and most of the music in all the folk song books on the market.

MUSICAL NOTATION

Musical tones are represented on the page by symbols called <u>Notes</u>. They appear on a a group of five horizontal lines called a <u>Staff.</u> The type of note indicates the <u>Time Value</u> and its position, <u>Pitch</u>. The types of notes used in this book with their comparative Time Values are:

> Whole note (o) = 2 Half notes (♩) = 2 Quarter notes (♩) =
> 2 Eighth notes (♪) = 2 Sixteenth notes (♪)

Eighth notes and sixteenth notes can be joined by beams. ♫

The pitch of notes is designated by the first seven letters of the alphabet.
In this book (which uses the treble cleff only) the pitches are:

Periods of silence (rests) have the same time values as the corresponding notes:

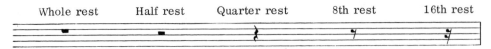

A <u>Dot</u> after a note or rest increases its time value by one-half.

Music is divided by vertical lines called <u>Bars</u> into portions called <u>Measures</u>.
The total time value for a measure is indicated by the time signature in the form of a
"fraction". The upper number indicates the number of counts (beats) per measure
and the lower number gives the time value of each beat.

A section of music to be played twice is indicated:

A sharp (♯) placed before a note raises its pitch by onehalf step.
A flat (♭) placed before a note lowers its pitch by onehalf step.
A natural (♮) cancels the sharp or flat.

The melodies for the songs in this book will be written out in music. However, to help
the student learn to read music painlessly, the names of the notes have been printed
over the notes in the musical staff for a portion of this book. Another simplification
that will be found in this book only is that the half and whole notes have been written
out as tied quarters to make counting the beat easier. In addition, dotted notes have
been written in a tied form to aid in determing where the beat goes. These are
indicated by being tied over the notes to distinguish from a slur.

Notice that the "thumb-brush" accompaniment we learned in the previous chapter consists of four quarter notes per measure. The thumb notes are the first and third
quarters and the two brushes are the second and fourth quarters of each measure.
Also, those mysterious vertical lines in the melody were the measure indications.

Now for a little practice. Below is written out
the melody to <u>Wildwood Flower</u> in music notation. Above the notes, in lower case type are
given the names of the notes indicated in the
music, <u>e</u>, <u>f</u>, <u>g</u>, <u>a</u>, <u>c</u>, <u>e</u>, etc. Below the notes
are the names of the chord bars to be played
that will allow that particular note to sound,
C, G7, C, F, C, etc. Each note is sounded with
the index finger picking toward the bass strings
of the 'harp in the vicinity of the note indicated,
as shown in Figure 9.

Figure #9

Notes can be located on the A-harp by looking under the strings at the piece of paper pasted on the autoharp. Here are given the names of the notes (and their places on the musical staff) which correspond to the string under which it is printed. If you don't have such a device on your autoharp, you can look up at the other end where the note names are printed near the tuning pegs. If you have the Appalachian model, which doesn't have anything printed on it, put the plastic thing for tuning the machine over the pegs and use that for a guide for playing. You can easily make a piece of paper with the note names on it in the right places and scotch tape it under the strings.

To play the first note of <u>Wildwood Flower</u>, hold down the C chord bar and use the index finger to sound the e string. You don't have to be too accurate with the index finger, just as long as you <u>do</u> sound that e string and no strings <u>higher</u> in pitch. You can sound a few strings <u>lower</u> in pitch than the melody note. The second note is played by changing to the G7 chord bar and picking the f note. Notice that the musical notation gives the "shape" of the melody, that is, the f note is placed higher on the staff than is the previous e note and thus the f note is higher in pitch than the e note and is found "higher" on the A-harp. This fact is most helpful in learning to play the A-harp since by observing the "shape of the melody" you know which way to move the index finger to pick the next note. In the first two notes of <u>Wildwood Flower,</u> e and f the index finger has to move very little, only one string.

The first note of the second measure is a g note obtained by depressing the C chord bar. This note is a half note (indicated by two quarter notes tied together; 1/4 + 1/4 = 1/2) and therefore receives two beats. The index finger picks once at the beginning of the note. The second beat is a rest for the index finger and that g note is allowed to "ring" on into the second beat. The index next plays the third beat, an a note using the F chord bar. The same rhythmic pattern is repeated for the next six measures. Notice that the letter name of the notes are printed only above the notes that the index finger sounds.

WILDWOOD FLOWER

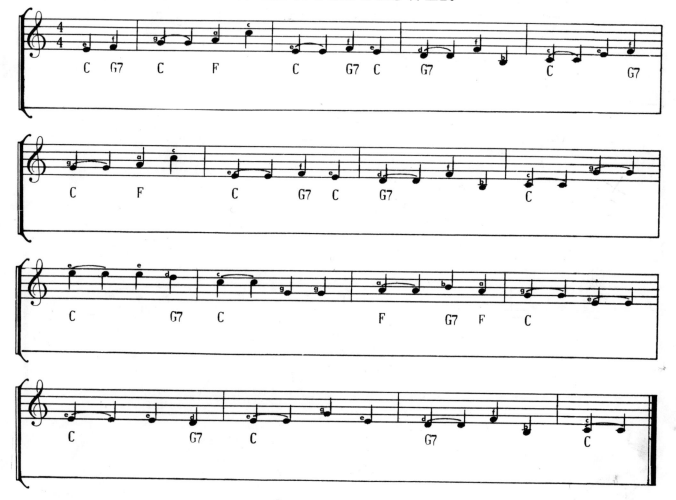

To get familiar with playing melody on the autoharp, we will try four more songs. The first, Red River Valley, has half notes in the second and third measures. Remember to play only the first quarter note and then let the note ring while the index finger is resting for the second beat of the half note. In the fourth measure, we have three quarter notes tied together. Again the index plays only once at the beginning of the figure and then rests for the two remaining beats. At the beginning of the fifth measure we have two rests, each being a quarter note long. Here you simply start playing on the third beat of the measure, resting for the first two. The last measure has a whole note (four quarters tied together), again we play once and let the note ring for the second, third and fourth beats of the measure.

RED RIVER VALLEY

In the second measure of <u>Lonesome Valley</u> is a whole note which is tied to the first beat of the next measure. Here we play the first quarter, as usual, then let the note ring on beats two, three, four, and one. We then resume playing on beat number two of the third measure. A pause in the melody which is longer than one or two beats is admittedly very boring, but be patient. In the next few chapters we will learn what to do about those pauses.

LONESOME VALLEY

The next two songs should provide the practice required to become confident in reading music and playing the melody on the autoharp.

BANKS OF THE OHIO

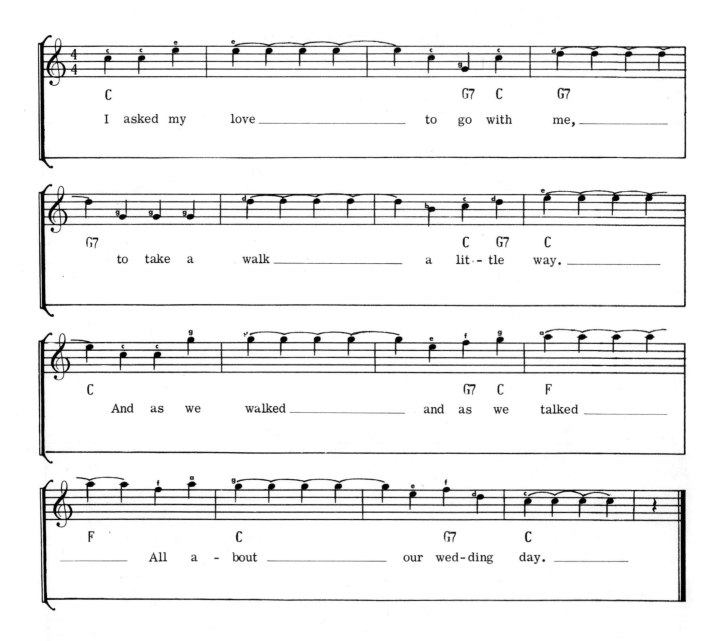

C I asked my love _____ to go with **G7 C** me, **G7**

G7 to take a walk _____ a lit-tle **C G7 C** way. _____

C And as we walked _____ and as we **G7 C** talked **F**

F _____ All a-bout _____ our wed-ding **G7 C** day. _____

Then only say that you'll be mine,
In no other arms entwine.
Down beside where the waters flow,
Down by the banks of the Ohio.

I held my knife against her breast,
In my arms she gently pressed,
Saying, "Please, don't murder me,
I'm unprepared for eternity."

I took her by her lily white hand,
Led her to the river strand,
I picked her up and I threw her in,
And I watched as she floated down.

I started home, twixt twelve and one,
Crying, Lord, what have I done?
I've murdered the girl I love
Because she would not marry me.

HARD AINT IT HARD

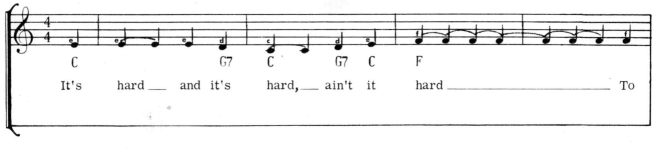

C   G7   C   G7   C   F

It's   hard   and it's   hard, ain't it   hard _____ To

C   F   C   G7

love one ___ who   ne - ver will be   true. _____ It's

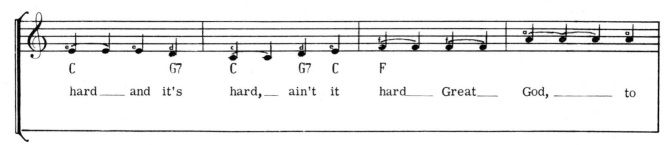

C   G7   C   G7   C   F

hard ___ and it's   hard, __ ain't it   hard___ Great___ God, _____ to

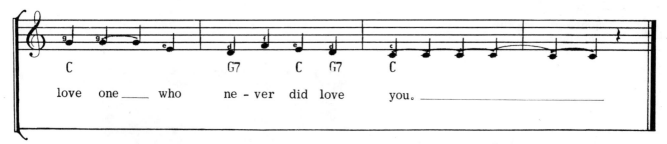

C   G7   C   G7   C

love one ___ who   ne - ver did love   you. _____

There is a place in this old town,
And that's where my true love lays around.
And she takes and sits on other knees,
To tell them things she'll never tell to me.

Don't go there a drinking and gambling.
Don't go there your sorrows for to drown.
That hark likker place is a low-down disgrace,
It's the meanest damn place in this town.

The first time I saw my true love,
She was standing by the bar-room door,
And the last time I saw her false-hearted
        smile
She was dead on that bar-room floor.

CHAPTER III-MELODY PICKING ON AUTOHARP

Now we come to the point where we are ready to play the melody and the accompaniment on the 'harp at the same time. We will be using both the thumb and index finger. Let us look at the first tune, Banks of the Ohio. There are now two parts written out, you will recognize the top part as the melody played by the index finger and the bottom part is similar to the thumb accompaniments we learned at the beginning of this book.

Let's play the melody line first. You will note that it is exactly the same as the one in the previous chapter, including those long, boring pauses. Now, as promised, we are going to do something about them.

Now let us look at the bass, or accompaniment part. Play through the bass part, treating the P's and the T's as just thumb notes for a while. The first measure consists of three thumb notes; the second measure is thumb, brush, thumb brush; the third measure is four thumb notes, the fifth measure is two thumb brush figures; etc. Not too different from the accompaniments we have been playing. But why all the thumb notes instead of the regular thumb-brush pattern? Because we are no longer accompanying the voice (a more or less independent instrument) we are now going to accompany our index finger, and a slightly different approach must be taken.

The melody played by the index and the accompaniment played by the thumb can be combined in the following way. We will play the first note of the melody of Banks of the Ohio, a c note using a C chord bar, at the same time that the thumb plays the first note of the accompaniment, the short thumb stroke. This is accomplished by the pinching motion of the index and thumb of the right hand. Therefore, the P in the bass line stand for "pinch." This is shown in Figure 10.

Figure #10

The second note is also a pinch, again a c note. The third note is again a pinch, but now on the e note of the C chord bar. The second measure begins with another pinch, again on the e note. This is followed by a brush by the thumb as the index finger rests. The third beat of the second measure is occupied by a thumb note alone without the index finger, which is still resting. This is indicated by the T, for the thumb alone. This is followed by another brush. And so on for the rest of the song. Be careful not to confuse the pinches, P, and the single thumb notes, T.

And those long pauses have been filled in.

BANKS OF THE OHIO

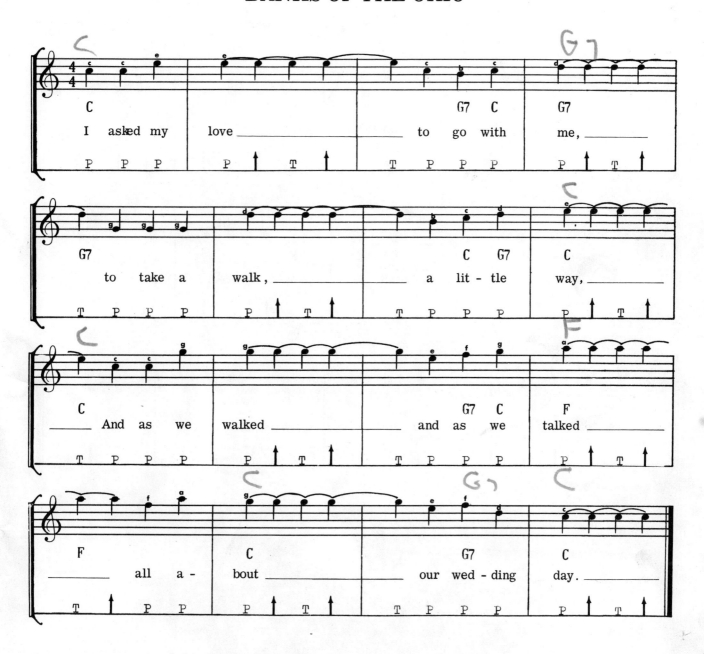

Below are given some more songs for practice, you have already learned to pick the melodies, so all that remains is to add the thumb to develop good solos.

HARD AINT IT HARD

It's hard and it's hard, ain't it hard To love one who never will be true. It's hard and it's hard, ain't it hard, Great God, To love one who never did love you.

RED RIVER VALLEY

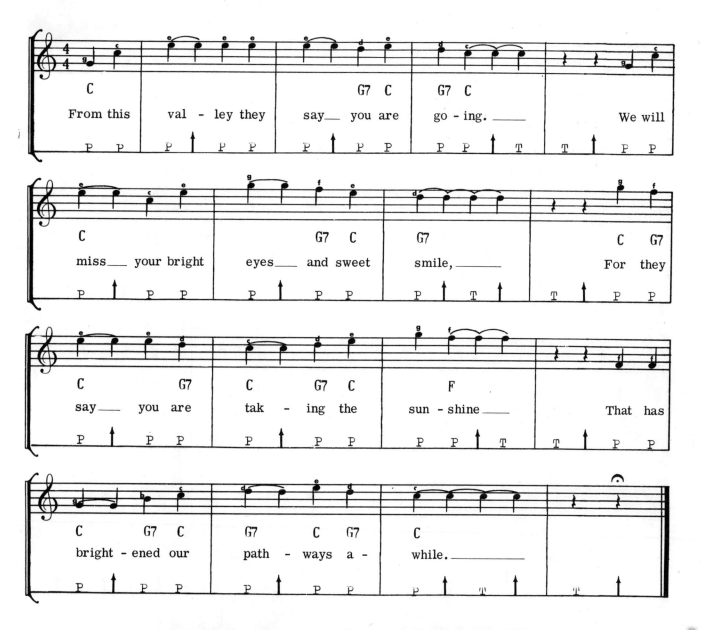

From this val - ley they say__ you are go - ing. ____ We will
miss__ your bright eyes__ and sweet smile, _____ For they
say__ you are tak - ing the sun - shine ____ That has
bright - ened our path - ways a - while. _____

LONESOME VALLEY

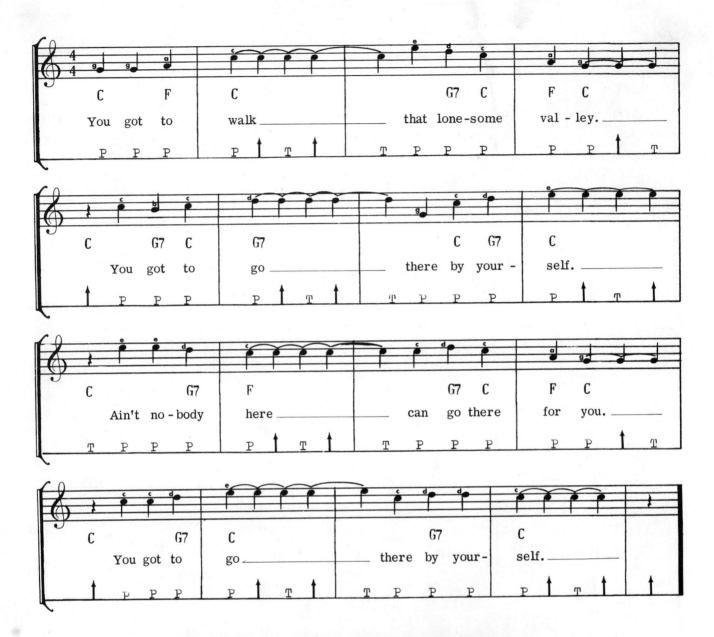

You got to walk that lonesome valley.
You got to go there by yourself.
Ain't nobody here can go there for you.
You got to go there by yourself.

WILDWOOD FLOWER

All the songs we have considered so far were in $\frac{4}{4}$ time (also known as march time). We will now learn to play songs in $\frac{3}{4}$ time (waltz time). As you can already read from the time signature itself, each measure consists of three beats, each beat being a quarter note long. The bass still consists of thumb notes and brush notes, but now the basic accompaniment is:

$\frac{3}{4}$ Thumb, Brush, Brush/Thumb, Brush, Brush/ etc.

Our next tune, <u>Wagoners Lad,</u> is in waltz time.

WAGONER'S LAD (3/4 TIME)

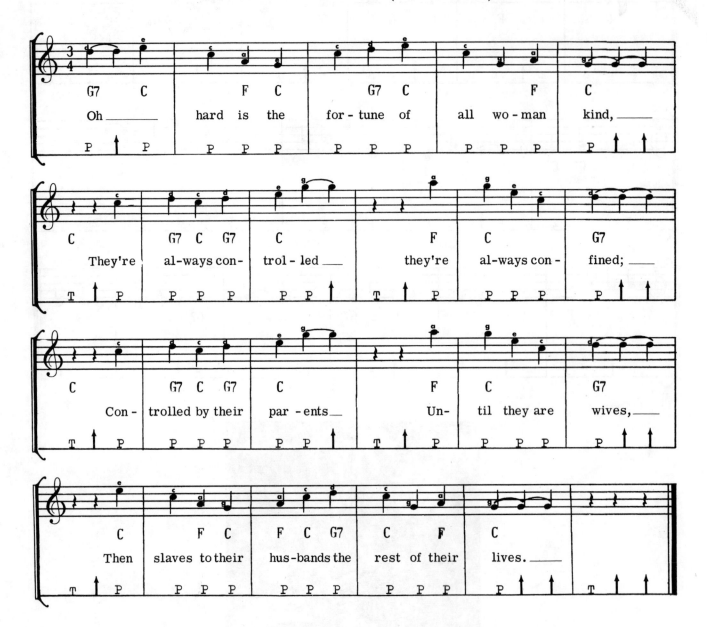

Oh, I am a poor girl, my fortune is sad,
I have always been courted by the wagoner's
lad;
He courted me daily, by night and by day,
And now he is loaded and going away.

Your parents don't like me because I am poor,
They say I'm not worthy of entering your
door;
I work for my living, my money's my own,
And if they don't like me they can leave me
alone.

Your horses are hungry, go feed them some
hay,
Come sit down beside me as long as you stay.
My horses ain't hungry, they won't eat your
hay,
So fare you well darling, I'll be on my way.

Your wagon needs greasing, your whip is to
mend,
Come sit down here by me as long as you can,
My wagon is greasy, my whip's in my hand,
So fare you well darling, no longer to stand.

CHAPTER IV - MORE CHORDS AND KEYS

In this chapter we will give some attention to developing the left hand, now that the right hand can play a number of melodies comfortably. You have probably noticed that so far all the songs in this book have used only three chords, the C, F, and G7 chord bars. These three chords comprise the key of C. We will now learn to play in two more keys, the key of G, consisting of the G, C, and D7 chord bars, and the key of F using the F, Bb, and C7 chord bars. Notice that some of the chords bars are used in several keys, the C bar is used in the keys of C and G, and the F bar is used in both the keys of F and C. Also notice that the C7 chord bar used in the key of F is not the same as the C chord bar used in the key of C. The chord bars comprising the keys are summarized in the table below.

Key	Chords				Key	Chords		
C	C	F	G7		A	A	D	E7
F	F	Bb	G7		Am	Am	Dm	E7
G	G	C	D7		Dm	Dm	Gm	A7

The first new key we will try will be the key of **G**. There is nothing difficult here except keeping track of the three new chord bars. To make this easier, we will start with a familiar tune, Wildwood Flower. You should start this song in the same way we have learned the other songs in this book, play the melody alone until it is comfortable, then add the thumb part.

WILDWOOD FLOWER (G)

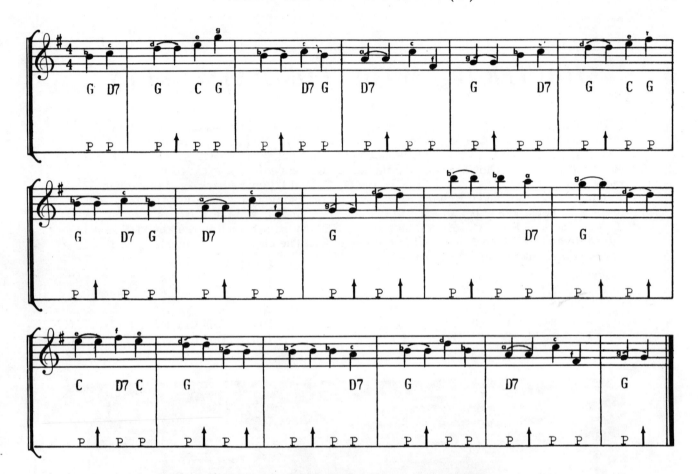

The next song in the key of G is a new tune, Bury Me Beneath the Willow, this should give enough practice to get familiar with the key of G.

BURY ME BENEATH THE WILLOW (G)

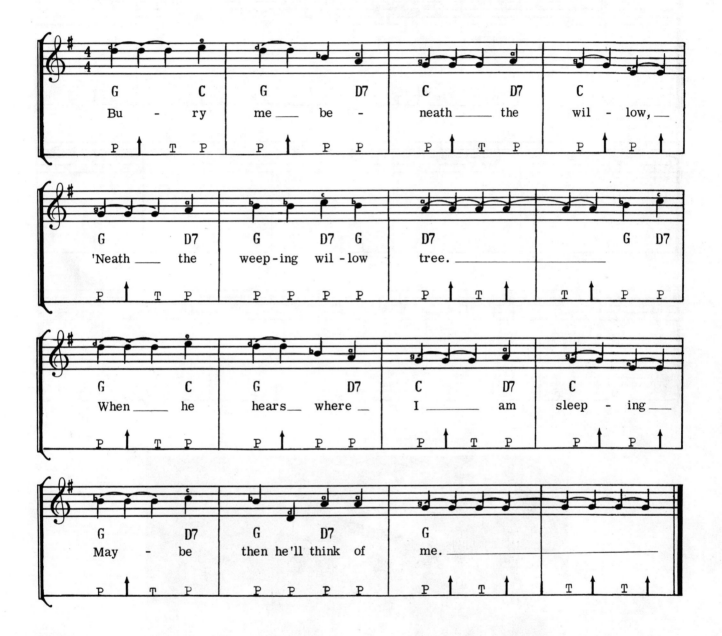

My heart is sad and I am lonely
Thinking of the one I love.
When will I see him, oh, no never
Until we meet in heaven above.

She told me that she dearly loved me
How could I believe her untrue.
Until an angel softly whispered,
"She has been untrue to you."

Tomorrow was to be our wedding,
Where, Oh Lord, can she be.
She's gone, she's gone to love another,
She no longer cares for me.

Now we will again play <u>Wildwood Flower</u>, but this time in the key of F, using the F, Bb, and C7 chord bars.

WILDWOOD FLOWER (F)

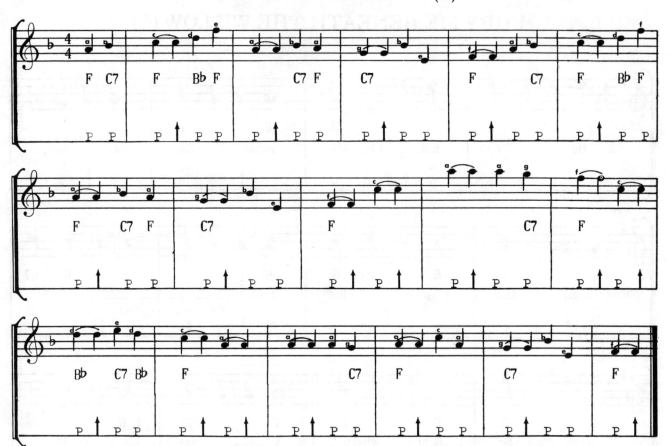

Our new keys, G, and F, can, of course, be used for many tunes in $\frac{3}{4}$ time as well as in $\frac{4}{4}$ time. Here is I Never Will Marry, a tune in waltz time and in the key of G.

I NEVER WILL MARRY (3/4 TIME, G)

New Words & New Music Arrangement by Mrs. Texas Gladden.
© Copyright 1958 MELODY TRAILS, INC., New York, N.Y.
Used By Permission

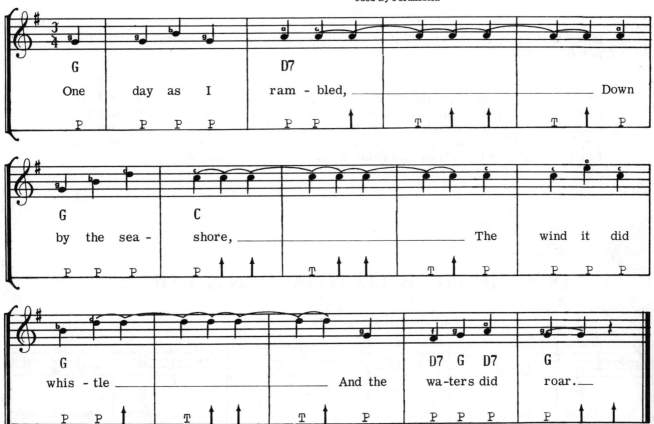

I spied a fair damsel,
Making pitiful sound,
It sounded so lonesome,
In the waters all 'round.

CHORUS:

I never will marry, I'll be no man's bride,
I expect to live single, all the days of my life.
The shells in the ocean, will be my death bed,
The fish in deep water, swim over my head.

My love's gone and left me, he's the one I
adore.
He's gone where I never shall see him no more.
She plunged her fair body, in the water so deep,
She closed her pretty blue eyes, in the waters
to sleep.

45

In addition to the three basic chords for each key that we have learned so far, other chords are sometimes used within a song. Here will be presented several examples.

The first is known as the "relative minor,"

Key	Relative Minor Chord
C	Am
G	Em
F	Dm

In our next song, Down In the Willow Garden, we shall be using the last one, the Dm in the key of F.

Now that we are using four chords we must plan to use our left hand so that we do not suddenly find ourselves without fingers left to play the next chord. I use the third finger for the F chord (holding the 'harp against the chest), the middle finger for both the C7 and the Dm (since, you will notice, in this tune the C7 is never followed by the Dm nor the Dm by the C7) and the index finger for the Bb chord bar.

DOWN IN THE WILLOW GARDEN (3/4 TIME, F)

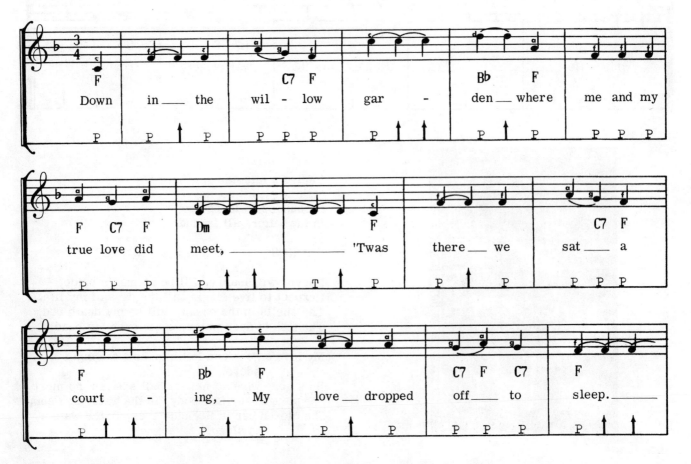

46

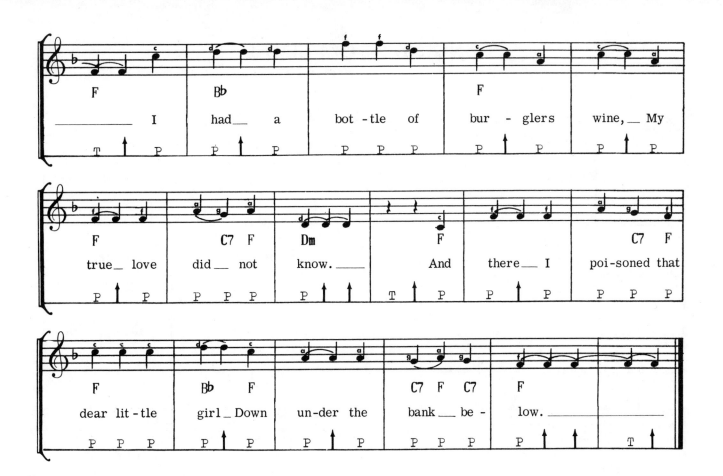

I stabbed her with my dagger,
Which was a bloody knife;
I threw her in the river,
Which was a dreadful sight,
My father often told me
The money would set me free,
If I would murder that dear little girl
They call Rose Connelly.

And now he sits in his cabin door,
A-wiping his weeping eye.
Waiting for his own true son
To die on the gallows high.
My race is run beneath the sun,
Cruel Hell's now waiting for me,
For I have murdered the girl I loved,
Whose name was Rose Connelly.

In addition to the relative minor chord, we shall look at two types of "passing chords."
The first, which occurs in Engine 143 is the use of a D7 in the key of C. * It is best to
play this chord bar with the little finger. In the other keys, similar chords are
possible which correspond to this passing chord (known as the II7 chord); these are
summarized in the table below.

Key	II7 chord	IV7 chord
C	D7	E7
G	A7	B7
F	G7	A7
A	B7	C#7

*The Carter Family did not use this chord progression in their recording of the song.
It has, however, become popular to insert the passing chord as shown in the music.
It is up to the performer to decide how close he should stick to "tradition."

ENGINE 143 (3/4 TIME)

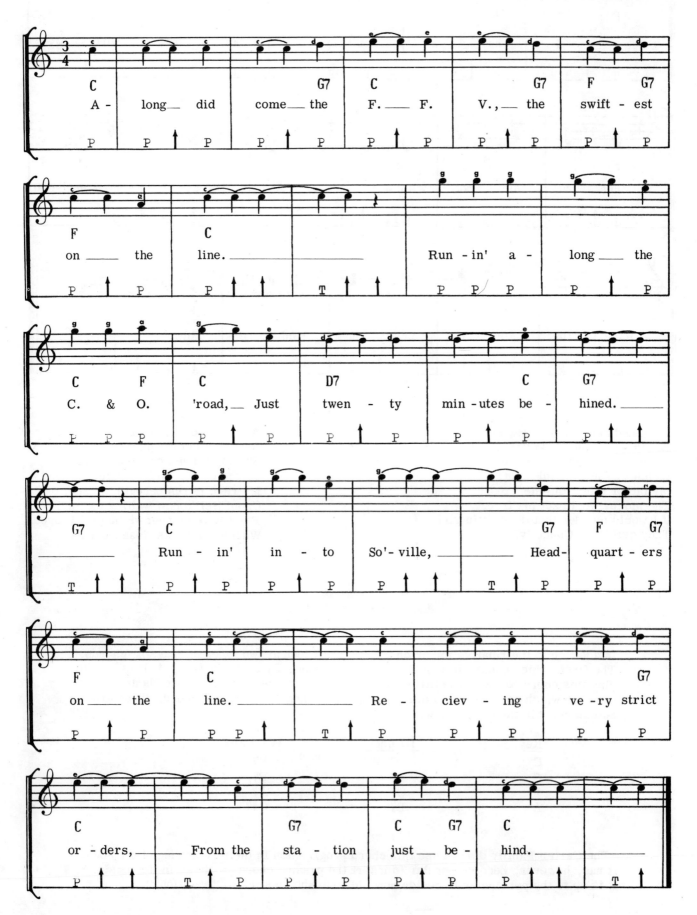

Georgie's mother come to him,
With a bucket on her arm.
Says, "My darlin' son
Be careful how you run.
For many a man has lost his life
In tryin' to make lost time.
And if you run your engine right
You'll get there just on time."

Up the road she darted
And into the rocks she crashed.
Upside down the engine turned
Poor Georgie's breast was mashed.
His head was against the firebox door,
The flames where rollin' high.
"I'm glad I was born an engineer
On the C. & O. road to die."

Doctor says to Georgie,
"My darlin' boy lie still.
You're life can yet be saved
If its God's blessed will."
"Oh, no," says George,
"That will not do
I want to die so free.
I want to die for the engine I love,
One hundred and forty three."

Doctor said to Georgie,
"Your life cannot be saved.
Murdered upon the railroad,
To lay in a lonesome grave."
His face was covered up with blood,
His eyes you could not see.
And the very last words that Georgie said
Was, "Nearer my God to Thee."

The second type of passing chord is the use of an E7 in the key of C. This occurs in Railroad Bill. The E7 chord bars is played by the second finger and the F bar following played by the index. This passing chord is known as the IV7.

RAILROAD BILL

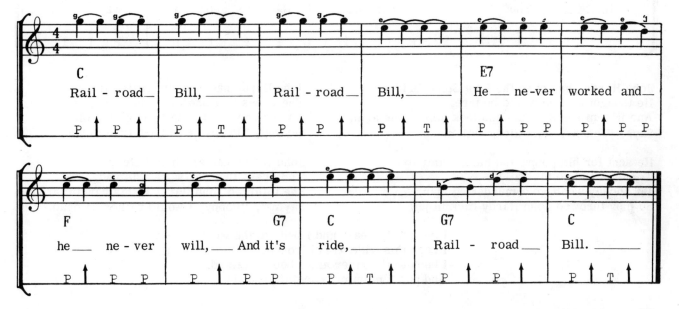

An unusual but very exciting chord progression occurs in John Hardy, where a Bb note is required. To get this Bb note one may use either a C7 chord bar or a Bb chord bar. I have chosen the latter for the arrangement given here. It is easiest to play the Bb chord bar with the side of the thumb of the left hand.

JOHN HARDY

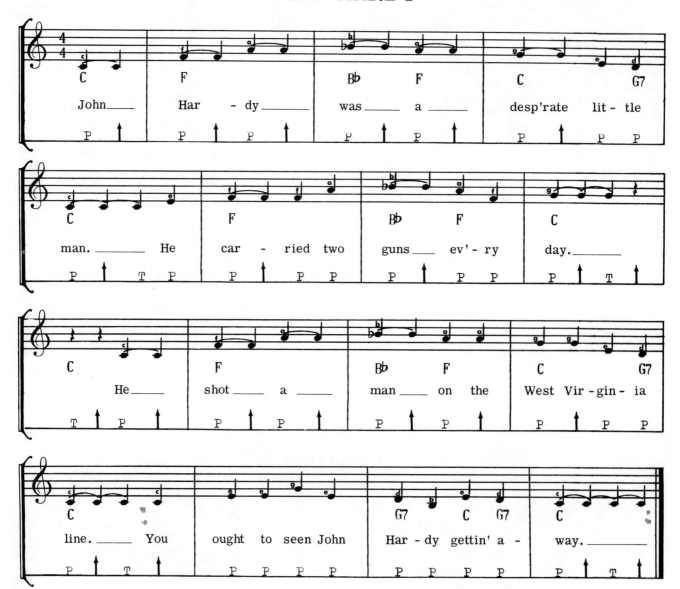

John Hardy, he got to the East Stone Bridge,
He thought that he would be free,
And it's up steps a man and took him by the arm,
Says, "Johnny, walk along with me."

He sent for his poppy and his mommy too,
To come and go his bail,
But money won't go a murdering man,
So they throwed John Hardy back in jail.

John Hardy had a pretty little girl,
The dress that she wore was blue,
As she come skipping through the old jail,
Saying', "Poppy, I've been true to you."

John Hardy had another little girl,
The dress that she wore was red;
She followed John Hardy to his hangin' ground
Saying', "Poppy, I would rather be dead."

I been to the east and I been to the west,
I been this wide world 'round.
I been to the river and I been baptized,
And now I'm on my hangin' ground.

CHAPTER V - OFF-BEATS AND SYNCOPATION

In this chapter we will return to the development of the right hand. So far all the melody notes that have been played by the right hand index finger have been played at the same times as the right hand thumb was playing a bass notes. In other words, all the melody notes that we have played have been in pinches. In this chapter we will investigate melody notes that are not played by pinches.

The thumb notes, both the short thumb notes and the brushes, outline the "beat" of the music. Therefore, all the melody notes that are played with the beat are called "on-beats." Similarly, all the melody notes that are not played on the beat are called "off-beats." Playing off-beats on the autoharp will raise various problems which must be solved. In this chapter we will look at several musical examples of off-beats and we will see how these problems can be solved.

For our introduction of off-beats, we will play Railroad Bill. This piece has been arranged to use only one off-beat pattern. Look at the first measure. Looking at the thumb part, you will notice that everything is familiar except for the figure representing the third beat. This figure means that the thumb plays a thumb note, T, on the third beat and the index finger next plays the g note after the third beat but before the fourth beat of the measure. The index finger note comes half way between the third and fourth beats of the measure. Thus for the first measure we have: Pinch, Brush, Thumb-Index, Brush. The count for the same notes would be 1, 2, 3, &, 4.

Now let us see how this figure is indicated in the music. In the first measure we have two quarter notes tied to an eighth note, followed by an eighth note tied to a quarter note. You can easily see that if we compare this to a normal measure to consist of four quarter notes, in this measure the third quarter notes has been split into two eighth notes; one has been tied to the first part of the measure and the second has been tied to the last note. The third beat comes on the first eighth note, as indicated in the count 1, 2, 3, &, 4. The thumb plays on 1, 2, 3, 4, and the index plays on the "&" note between the third and fourth beats.

This pattern of Pinch, Brush, Thumb-Index, Brush, is repeated several times in this arrangement of Railroad Bill. Once you have learned this pattern, you should try to put the off-beat note played by the index finger after the first, second and fourth beats also.

RAILROAD BILL

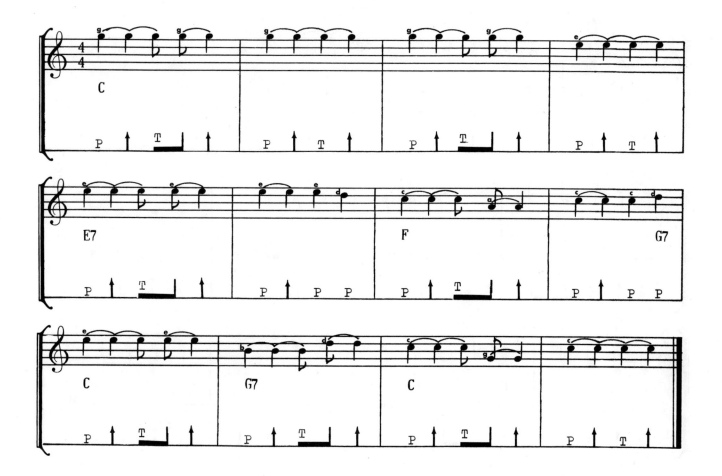

In the Golden Vanity we find off-beats not only after the third beat, but now after the first, second and fourth beats also.

In the second measure, for instance, the off-beat follows the second beat. The count is 1, 2, &, 3, 4. Notice that the index finger note now follows a brush with the thumb: Pinch, Brush-Index, Pinch, Pinch. This requires a lot of work from the index finger since it must follow a single index note with a pinch, that is, it is playing two consecutive eighth notes, something new.

In the third measure we have the off-beat eighth note placed after the fourth beat. Here the off-beat comes after the fourth beat and before the first beat of the next measure. The count would be 1, 2, 3, 4, &, 1, 2, etc. The figures are as follows: Pinch, Brush, Thumb, Pinch-Index; Pinch, etc. Here the index finger is required to play three notes in succession: Pinch-Index, Pinch.

Later in this song we find the off-beat placed after the first beat: Pinch-Index, Brush, Thumb, Brush. The count is 1, &, 2, 3, 4. This should offer very little difficulty after working through the second and third measures.

Notice that the index finger is no longer "tied down" to the thumb as it was in the previous chapter. It is much freer and can play notes almost wherever it wants (or, rather, where ever you want it to). This freedom will be further explored in the following songs.

GOLDEN VANITY (F)

She had not been out but two weeks or three
When she was overtaken by the Turkish Revelee
As she sailed upon the low and lonesome low
As she sailed upon the lonesome sea.

Then up spake our little cabin boy
Saying, "What will you give me if I will them destroy,
If I sink them in the low and lonesome low
If I sink them in the lonesome sea?"

"Oh, the man that them destroys," our
        Captain then replied,
"Five thousand pounds and my daughter for his
        bride,
If he sinks them in the low and lonesome low
If he sinks them in the lonesome sea."

Then the boy smote his breast and down
        jumped he,
He swum till he came to the Turkish Revelee,
As she sailed upon the low and lonesome low,
As she sailed upon the lonesome sea.

He had a little tool that was made for the use,
He bored nine holes in her hull all at once.
And he sunk her in the low and lonesome low
He sunk her in the lonesome sea.

He swum back to his ship and he beat upon the
        side,
Cried, "Captain pick me up for I'm wearied
        with the tide
And I'm sinking in the low and lonesome low
"I am sinking in the lonesome sea."

"No! I'll not pick you up," the Captain then
        replied
"I will shoot you, I will drown you, I will sink
        you in the tide,
I'll sink you in the low and lonesome low,
I will sink you in the lonesome sea."

"If it was not for the love that I bear for your
        men,
I would do unto you as I did unto them,
I would sink you in the low and lonesome low,
I would sink you in the lonesome sea."

Then the boy bowed his head and down sunk he
Farewell, farewell to the Golden Vanity,
As she sails upon the low and lonesome low,
As she sails upon the lonesome sea.

KEEP ON THE SUNNY SIDE

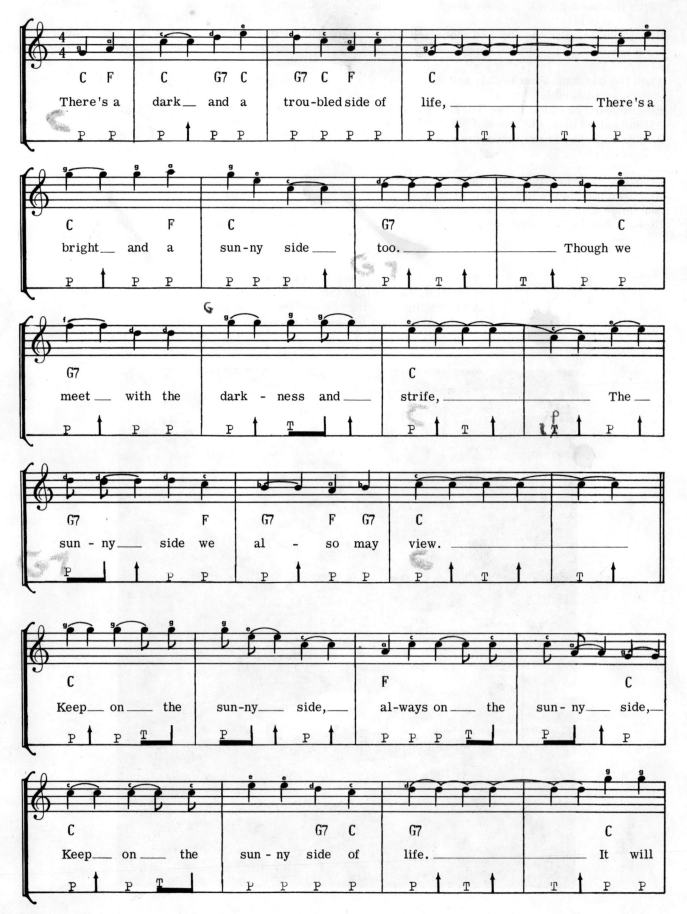

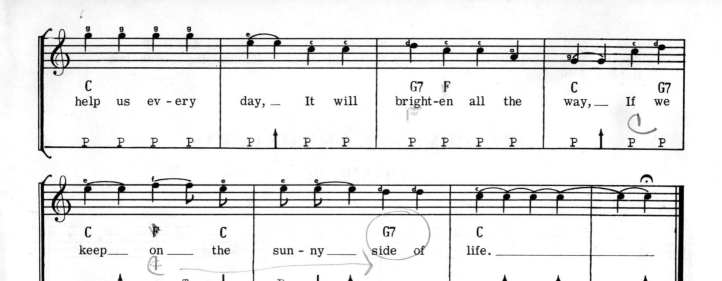

Oh, the storm and its fury break each day,
Crushing hopes that we cherish so dear;
Clouds and storms will in time pass away,
The sun again will shine bright and clear.

Let us greet with a song of hope each day,
Though the moment be cloudy or fair;
Let us trust in our Saviour away,
Who keepeth everyone in His care.

ROSEWOOD CASKET (G)

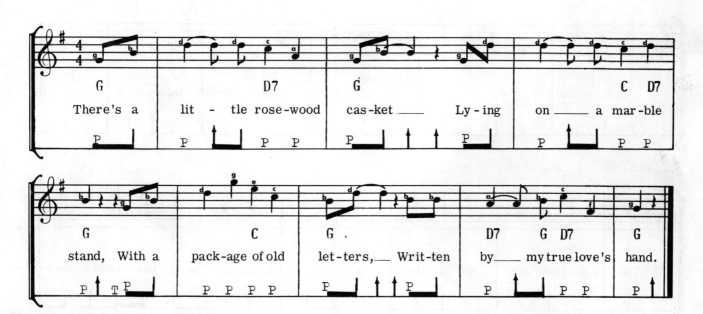

Come and sit beside me, sister,
Come and sit upon my bed,
Come and lay your head upon my pillow,
For my aching heart falls dead.

Last Sunday I saw him walking
With a lady by his side,
And I thought I heard him tell me,
She could never be his bride.

When I'm dead and in my coffin
And the shroud's around me bound,
And my narrow grave is ready
In some lonesome churchyard ground.

Take his letters and his locket,
Place together o'er my heart,
But the golden ring he gave me,
From my finger never part.

Now let us look at off-beats in $\frac{3}{4}$ time. Our first song is The Storms Are On The Ocean. This is not difficult except for the off-beats while changing chords toward the end of the song.

THE STORMS ARE ON THE OCEAN
(3/4 TIME, F)

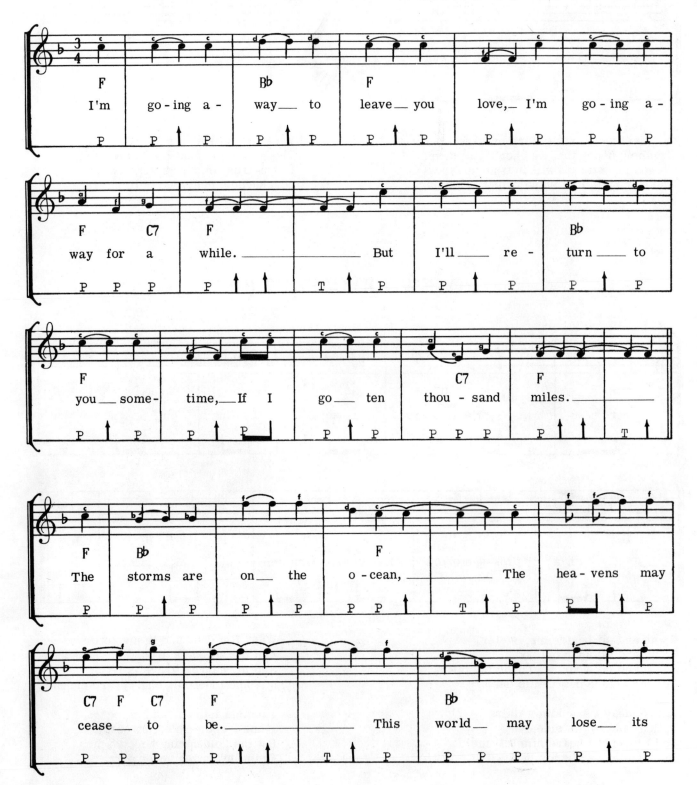

58

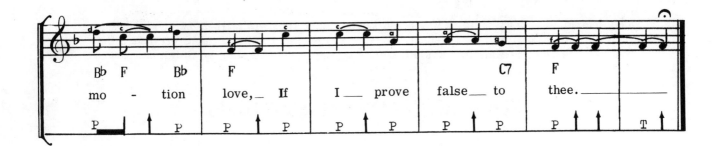

mo- tion | love,__ If | I __ prove | false__ to | thee.__

Oh, who will shoe your pretty little foot,
Oh, who will glove your hand?
And who will kiss your rosy cheeks,
When I'm in a far off land?

Oh, have you seen those mournful doves,
That fly from pine to pine?
A-mournin' for their own true loves
Just like I mourn for mine.

The second song in $\frac{3}{4}$ time is Forsaken Love. Here there is still more chord changing between the on-beat and the off-beat. Learn it slowly at first and make very sure that the changes and off-beats are smooth before trying to get the song up to tempo.

FORSAKEN LOVE (3/4 TIME, F)

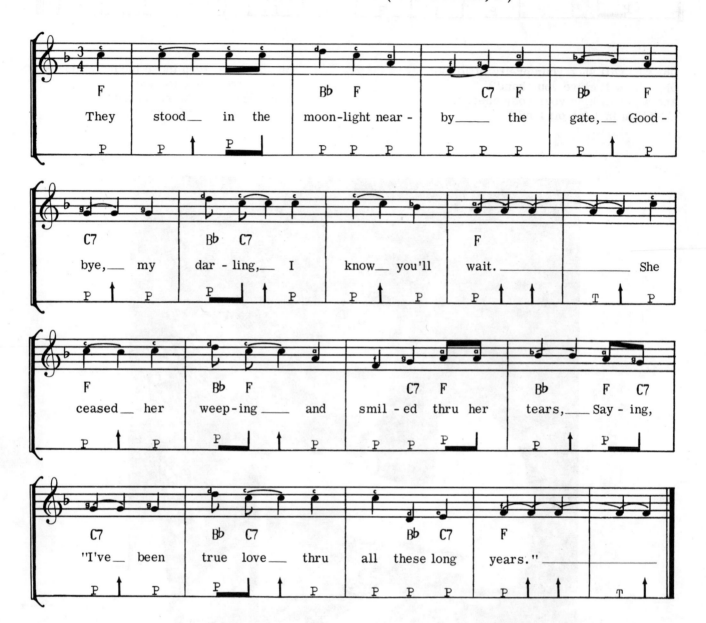

For on tomorrow at the break of day,
He was to journey so far away;
He held her closer, his promised bride,
And to her questions, these words replied.

I've loved you always, yet, I've been true,
My heart shall never be loveless for you;
Oh, darling, believe me, far over the sea,
Thru life or death, so faithful I'll be.

If we can put in off-beats to correspond to the melody line of a song, we can also leave them out!!! Our next song, Black Jack David, illustrates this quite well. Look at the first measure. To play the melody as written the figures would be, Pinch, Pinch, Pinch-Index, Pinch-Index. Aside from being difficult, it doesn't sound quite right for this song. Simplifying the first measure to four pinches makes the song easier to play and it sounds better. This simplifying maneuver can be seen throughout this song, though there are still a sufficient number of off-beats to make it interesting and challenging. Try this same thing with some of the previous songs that we have learned, you'll find that some very interesting variation can be found this way.

Also, don't let that measure of $\frac{6}{4}$ time in the middle of the song bother you. This simply means that there are six quarter notes in this measure instead of the usual four. The result is that the Dm chord is held longer than it would be if the measure were in $\frac{4}{4}$ time. You can hold it even longer than is indicated if you wish by simply adding more $\frac{4}{4}$ thumb-brush figures.

BLACK JACK DAVID (F)

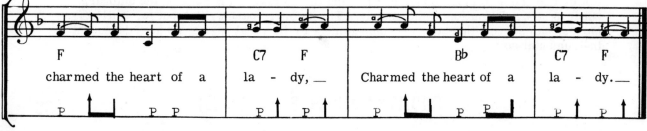

How old are you my pretty little miss,
How old are you my honey?
She answered him with a silly grin,
"I'll be sixteen next Sunday, (2X)

Come go with me my pretty little miss,
Come go with me my honey,
I'll take you 'cross the deep blue sea
Where you'll never want for money. (2X)

She pulled off her high-heeled shoes,
All made of Spanish leather.
She put on those low-heeled shoes
And they rode off together. (2X)

Last night I lay on a warm feather bed
Beside my husband and baby.
But tonight I lay on the cold, cold ground
By the side of Black Jack David. (2X)

It will be immediately apparent to most guitar players that there is a strong relation between guitar fingerpicking and the material presented in this chapter. In fact, many good autoharp players are also excellent guitarists, Maybelle Carter, Mike Seeger, Peggy Seeger, Doc Watson, to name a few. Therefore it is highly recommended that the autoharp students pursue a parallel study of guitar fingerpicking styles. Appropriate references are listed in the bibliography.

CHAPTER VI -
DEVELOPMENT OF INSTRUMENTAL SOLOS

In the last chapter we learned how to use off-beats in various places in the melody. We also learned that we could, if we wanted, leave out certain notes of the melody, especially if they were just repeats of the notes just sounded and if they followed very quickly one after the other. In this chapter we will see examples of notes added to the melody line in order to develop instrumental solos.

The first thing we will learn is one more type of note that the index finger will play. This is a brush downward from the treble strings to the bass strings and is indicated by an arrow pointing downward. This is very similar to the single note except that the stroke is long. In addition it doesn't have any assigned pitch, though it will sound best if it is the same or lower pitch than the index note previously played. In other words, it's just like an index note except sloppier.

In our first song of this chapter, Little Moses, we use the index brushes to substitute for the consecutive c notes in the second measure. In the fourth measure they are used to add interest to a long note. They can be used in that way in many of our previous songs.

Notice that the solo is no longer just playing the melody of the song on the autoharp, but it is now a derivation of the melody. The autoharp part written out for Little Moses, can serve either as an accompaniment to the vocal part or as an independent instrumental solo.

LITTLE MOSES (3/4 TIME)

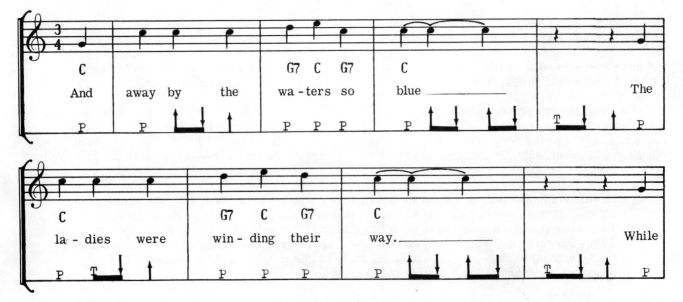

And away by the waters so blue
The infant was lonely and sad.
She took him in pity and thought him so pretty
And it made little Moses so glad.

    She called him her own, her beautiful son,
    And she sent for a nurse that was near. (2X)

And away by the waters so blue
They carried that beautiful child.
To his tender mother, his sister and brother
Little Moses looked happy and smiled.

    His mother so good, did all that she could
    To raise him and teach him with care. (2X)

And away by the sea that was red
Little Moses the servant of God.
While in him confided, the seas was divided
As upwards he lifted his rod.

    And the Jews safely crossed while Pharaoh's host
    Was drowned in the waters and lost. (2X)

And away on a mountain so high,
The last that he ever did see.
With Israel victorious his hopes were most glorious
That soon all the Jordan be free.

    When his spirit did cease, he departed in peace
    And rested in the heavens above. (2X)

We will now investigate another way in which an instrumental solo can vary from the
melody line of the song. In the first few songs we learned we played only the notes
that corresponded to the sung melody line. In the past few songs, we have added or
subtracted notes so that the tune would sound better on the autoharp. In our next tune,
another version of <u>Railroad Bill</u>, we depart still further from the sung melody. We
are now adding notes that do not occur in the melody line at all.

For instance, the c note in the first measure and the e note in the second measure do not correspond to anything that would be sung with Railroad Bill. These notes embellish or ornament the bare melody line. In general, you will find that the ornament notes that sound the best are in the same chord as the melody note itself. Therefore, they can usually be obtained without changing chord bars.

RAILROAD BILL

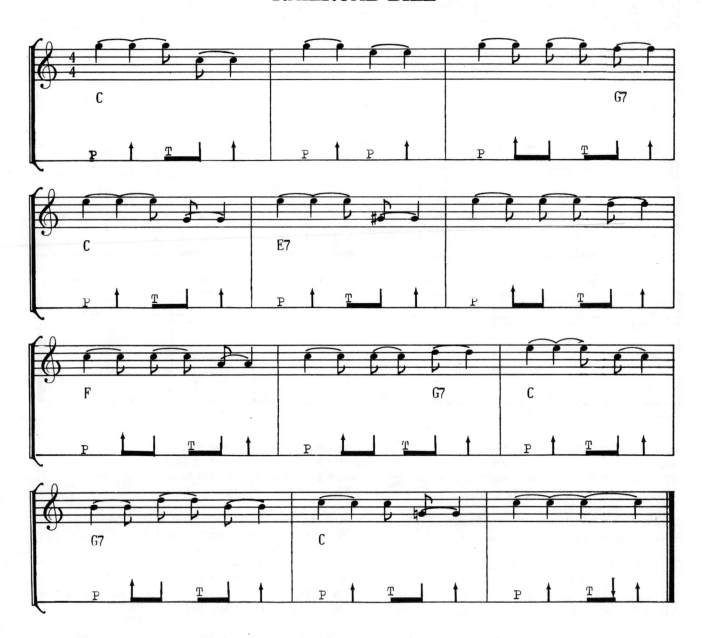

In our final song of this chapter, Man of Constant Sorrow, we get to an instrumental solo that is rather complicated. I have tried to annotate here approximately what can be played. The student should feel perfectly free to improvise his own solo once he can confidently play the melody of the song. A solo of this type should not be memorized. Rather the techniques used for developing such a solo should be at hand and the melody should be familiar to the player. With this knowledge the instrumentalist should be able to produce a similar or (hopefully) better solo. I, personally, would be hard pressed to play a solo such as this twice exactly the same way.

MAN OF CONSTANT SORROW

For six long years I've been in trouble,
No pleasure here on earth I've found,
For in this world I'm bound to ramble,
I've got no friends to help me now.

It's fare you well my own true lover,
I never expect to see you again,
For I'm bound to ride that northern railroad,
Perhaps I'll die upon this train.

You may bury me in some deep valley,
For many years where I may lay,
Then you may learn to love another,
While I am sleeping in my grave.

Maybe your friends think I'm just a stranger,
My face you will never see no more,
But there is one promise that is given,
I'll meet you on God's golden shore.

CHAPTER VII - WORKING FROM SONG BOOKS

Much of the material that you will be working with on the autoharp will come from song books. Working from written sources, sources not specifically written for the autoharp, will present special difficulties and problems. We will deal with some of them in this chapter.

The first problem is that of key. The autoharp will play in a very limited number of keys. If we find a song in the key of Eb or in C# or in some other mystic key, we must do something to be able to play it on the autoharp. This something is a very simple musical trick with the awesome name of "transposing." Transposing is as easy as counting up to twelve (literally). The techniques of transposing allow you to change the melody and chords of a song from any existing key to any key you desire. The easiest way to see how it works is to do some examples.

Let us pick a song from a song book. Pack Up Your Sorrows by Dick Farina was published in the February-March 1966 issue of Sing Out! magazine. This is typical of the sources for songs for the autoharp. The verse is reproduced below as it was published.

PACK UP YOUR SORROWS

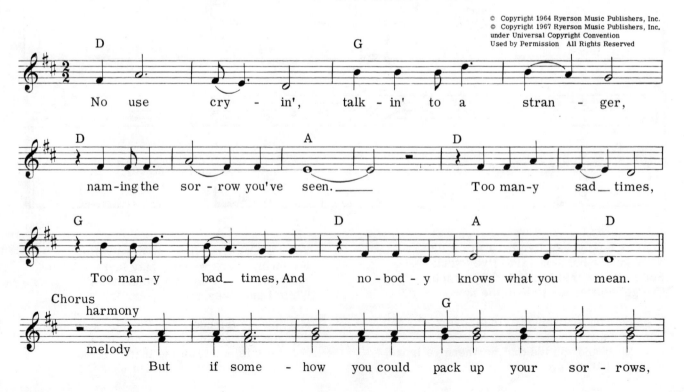

And give them all to me;_____ You would lose them,

I know how to use them, Give them all to me._____

No use rambling, walking in the shadows,
Trailing a wandering star.
No one beside you, no one to hide you,
And nobody knows where you are.

No use gambling, running in the darkness,
Looking for a spirit that's free.
Too many wrong times, too many long times,
And nobody knows what you see.

No use roaming, lying by the roadside,
Seeking a satisfied mind,
Too many highways, too many byways,
And nobody's walking behind!

This tune is in the key of D. There are two ways that you can determine the key in which a tune has been written. The tune will usually end on the note and at the chord corresponding to the name of the key. This song ends on a d note and with a D chord and it is in the key of D. But this is not always the case, there are exceptions to this system. The safest way to tell the key of a song is from the "key signature." The key is indicated by the number of sharps and flats at the beginning of each musical staff. This tune has two sharps and thus is in the key of D. For your reference, below is given a chart of the most common keys with their corresponding key signatures.

Key	Signature
C	No sharps or flats
G	one sharp
D	two sharps
A	three sharps
E	four sharps
F	one flat
Bb	two flats

Now let us transpose this song from the key of D to a key found on the autoharp, say, the key of F. That is, from the key of two sharps to the key of one flat. The easiest way to do this is to use the "chromatic scale" given below.

A, A#, B, C, C#, D, D#, E, F, F#, G, G#, A, A#, B, etc.

Notice that every note can be sharped but B and E. The scale repeats indefinitely. To transpose from the key of D to the key of F, let us count the number of half steps between D and F. Now, D to D# is one, D# to E is two and E to F is three. Therefore, D is three half steps below F, and, conversely F is three half steps above D. This means that if we raise every note of the melody in the key of D by three half steps, it will be in the key of F.

The first note of the melody is f#. The f note is sharped by the sharp in the key signature. Counting up three half steps in the chromatic scale will give the equivalent note in the key of F: f# to g, g to g#, g# to a! The corresponding note in the key of F is a! In the same way the note corresponding to a, the second note of the melody, can be found (c). Thus we can transpose the whole tune by placing each note three half steps higher into the key of F, as has been done in the example below. Notice that the chords have been "transposed" in the same way as the notes.

PACK UP YOUR SORROWS

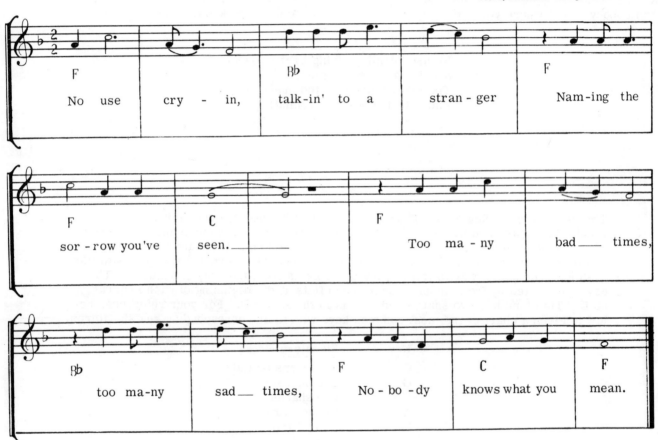

Now let us make some modifications on the music to make it easier to play on the autoharp. First, let us look at the time signature. It is in $\frac{2}{2}$ time. Each measure consists of two half notes, each getting one beat. It is easier to play in $\frac{4}{4}$ time where each quarter note gets one beat. No changes are necessary in the music to accomplish this since $\frac{4}{4}$ and $\frac{2}{2}$ differ only by the number of beats per measure. Next let us change the dotted notes and the long notes into their basic elements so that it is easier to see where the beat goes in each measure. This version is given below.

68

PACK UP YOUR SORROWS

F — No use _____ cry - in', ____ C7 F talk-in' to a _____ Bb stran - ger ____ C7 Bb

Bb F Nam-ing the ____ sor - row you've C7 seen. _____

C7 F Too ma-ny C7 F bad ____ times, ____ Bb too ma - ny ____ C7 sad _____ Bb C7 times, ____ Bb

Bb F No - bo - dy C7 knows ____ what you F C7 F mean. _____

You will notice that if you try to pick the melody with the chords given you will not be able to get all the notes. For instance, you won't be able to play the g note in the second measure while holding down the F chord bar. What chord bar should one use? To answer this question, one must know which notes are in which chords. Below is a table of the various chords and the notes that they contain.

Chord	Notes that the Chord Contains		Chord	Notes that the Chord Contains
C	C, E, G		D7	D, F#, A, C
G	G, B, D		E7	E, G#, B, D
F	F, A, C		A7	A, C#, E, G
Bb	Bb, D, F		Am	A, C, E
C7	C, E, G, Bb		Dm	D, F, A
G7	G, B, D, F		Gm	G, Bb, D

Knowing that the key of F uses the chords F, Bb and C7, we can see from the chart above that the only way of obtaining that g note in the second measure is to use a C7 chord, since neither the F or the Bb chords contain the g note. For the very next note, the f note, we must return to the F chord bar. The next note that presents a problem is the c note in the fourth measure. Notice that we can use either the F or the C7 chord bars. The best non-technical way of deciding which one to use is to play them both and use the one that sounds best. This has been done in the version above.

The next step is to add the thumb part and let the index finger play the simple melody. This has been done and is given below. Notice that even here it is not strictly mechanical and certain decisions must be made. The first measure, for instance, could be arranged in several ways: Pinch, Pinch, Brush, Thumb, or Pinch, Pinch, Thumb, Brush, etc. It is for the arranger to decide which of the possible patterns will fit the particular song in the best way.

PACK UP YOUR SORROWS

The next step is to turn the simple melody into an autoharp solo. This will be done by subtracting notes, adding ornaments and other devices. This step is strictly personal. No two artists will arrange the same tune in the same way. I have given my interpretation below.

PACK UP YOUR SORROWS

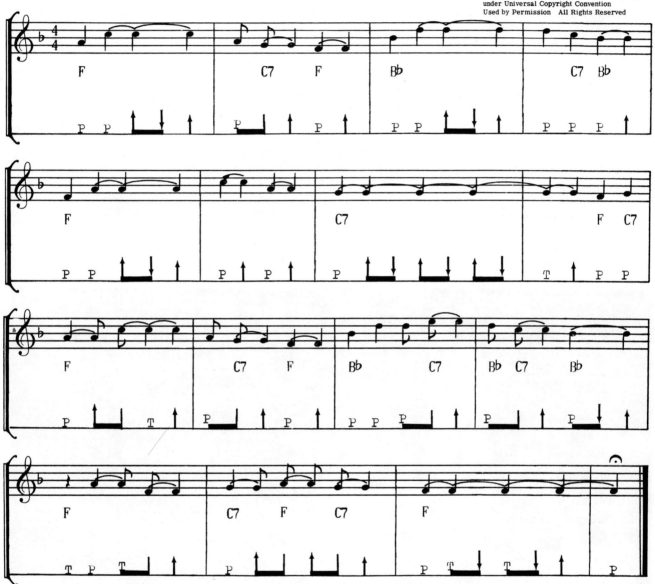

You will have noticed by now that the chorus of this song has not been arranged for the autoharp. It is simpler to work with than the verse which has been worked out in detail and therefore is left as an exercise to the student.

As a review of this chapter, the steps in arranging a song for the a-harp from a song book are given below:

1. Determine the key of the song
2. Choose a key for the song with the a-harp
3. Transpose the melody into the desired key
4. Change the time signature for easier playing
5. Add a simple bass line
6. Determine additional chord changes necessary
7. Derive final arrangement by additions, deletions and ornaments

CHAPTER VIII - SOME FANCY SOLOS

In this chapter we have four songs that are rather difficult. The first song is White Cockade which was originally a fiddle tune but has recently been played on banjo. The version given here is a note-for-note transcription of the fiddle tune. A high degree of coordination between the chording hand and the picking hand is required to play the long runs. Notice that the chords do <u>not</u> change with every note in the long runs.

WHITE COCKADE

In the second tune, Grandfather's Clock, we have several passing chords, an Am and a D7. In addition we have two measures in which the first quarter note is a pinch and the remaining three quarters are rests. The pinched note should not be allowed to ring for the rest of the measure, it should be damped or stopped from ringing. This is done by pushing down on the other two chord bars of the key, for instance, you pinch the c note in the C chord on the first beat, on the second beat you push down, in addition to the C chord bar, the F and the G7 chord bars and this stops all the strings from ringing. After picking the d note in the G7 chord bar, push down on the C and F chord bars to damp the note. This particular arrangement has no off-beats in it; I have left it to the student to arrange it as he sees fit.

GRANDFATHER'S CLOCK

In the next song, Pretty Peggy-O, difficulty is encountered in two ways, the number of chords that are used and the complexity of the picking required of the right hand. When holding the 'harp against the chest, play the Dm with the second finger and then you can reach the Am with the little finger. The following Bb chord can be reached in the usual way with the index finger. A little more complicated maneuver is required in the next phrase. The C7 is played with the middle finger, the Dm with the third finger, the F with the middle finger, the C7 with the index finger and then back to the F chord bar with the third finger.

PRETTY PEGGY-O

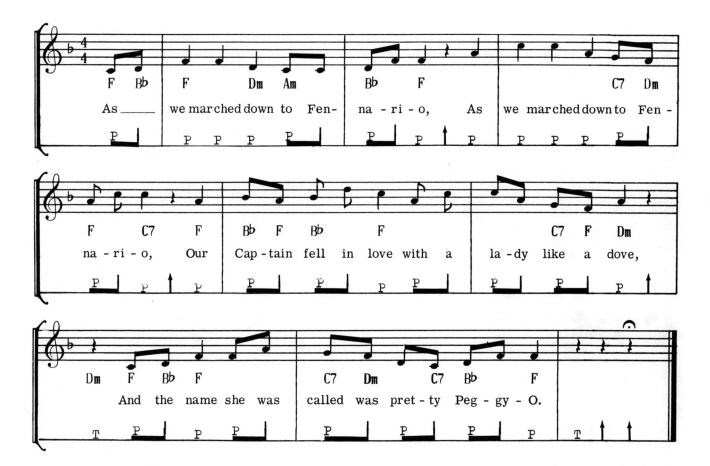

"Come go along with me, Pretty Peggy-O (2X)
In coaches you shall ride with your true love by
　your side,
Just as grand as any lady in the areo."

"What would your mother think, Pretty
　Peggy-O (2X)
What would your mother think for to hear the
　guineas clink,
And the soldiers all are marching before ye-o."

"You're the man that I adore, handsome
　Willy-O (2X)
You're the man that I adore, but your fortune
　is too low,
I'm afraid my mother would be angry, oh."

"Come a-trippin' down the stair, Pretty
　Peggy-O (2X)
Come a-trippin' down the stair and tie up your
　yellow hair,
Bid a last farewell to handsome Willy-o."

"If ever I return, Pretty Peggy-O (2X)
If ever I return the city I will burn,
And destroy all the ladies in the areo!"

"Our captain he is dead, Pretty Peggy-O (2X)
Our captain he is dead and he died for a maid,
And he's buried in the Louisiana Country-o."

In the last song, <u>Bully of the Town,</u> the Bb chord in the second measure must be played with the thumb. It is also easier to get the A7 with the thumb after playing the E7 with the index. The same is true of the C7 later in the song.

BULLY OF THE TOWN

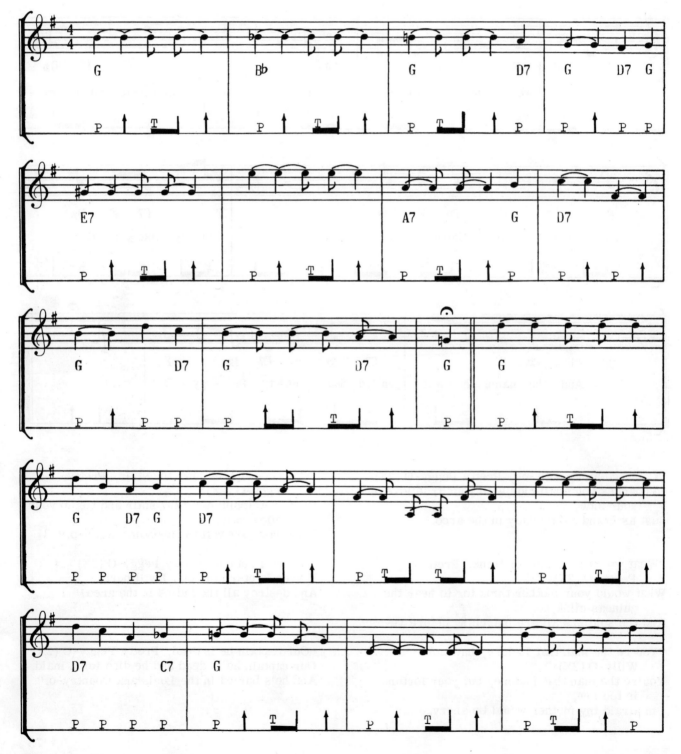

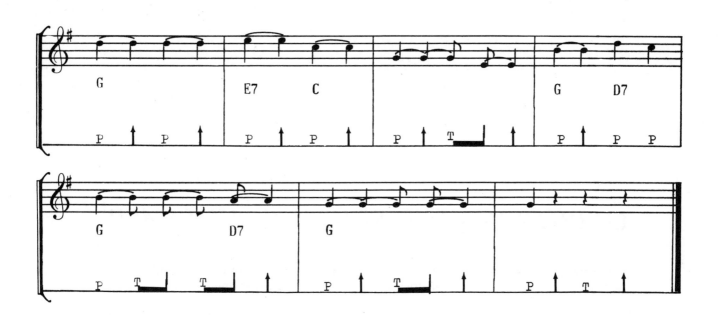

The material presented in this chapter should provide guidelines for your own arrangements of songs. Remember the more complicated arrangement is not necessarily the better one, and the faster you play does not necessarily mean the better you play.

CHAPTER IX - EXPERIMENTAL AUTOHARP

In addition to the techniques we have studied so far, a number of others can be used. These are not "traditional," therefore I have called them experimental.

The first of these is the imitation of the modal sound which is achieved on banjo by playing in the Mixolidian mode, that is, using only the chords G and F, or C and D. A tune that is in this mode is Little Maggie. The chords that are used on the autoharp are the C chord bar and a combination of the D7 and the Dm chord bars held down at the same time to produce a partial chord. The tune is not difficult and the results are very interesting.

LITTLE MAGGIE

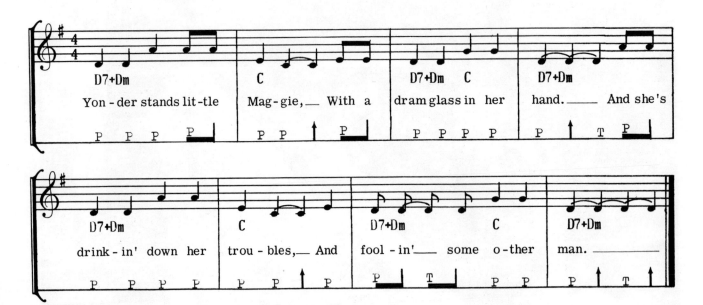

Tell me how could I ever stand it,
Just to see those two blue eyes.
They're shining like the diamonds,
Like the diamonds in the sky.

Sometimes I have a nickel,
And sometimes I have a dime.
And it's sometimes I have ten dollars,
Just to pay Little Maggie's fine.

Well the first time I seen Little Maggie
She was sitting by the banks of the sea.
Had a forty-five strapped around her shoulder,
And a banjo on her knee.

Now she's marching down to the station,
Got a suitcase in her hand.
She's going for to leave me,
She's going to some far distant land.

Another technique which has not been discussed so far is the hammer. To achieve this effect, pick the 'harp with a Pinch without holding down a chord bar, then, immediately after the pinch, push down on a chord bar. This eliminates all the "bad" notes leaving only the notes in the chord. This is used by Maybelle Carter on her recording of Foggy Mountain Top, recorded with Flatt and Scruggs.

The hammer can be played with the thumb alone. This produces almost a slur up into the melody note which is similar to the Southern Appalachian vocal style. Several traditional 'harp players use this technique.

Another experiment to perform is to cut your own chord bars for the A-harp. Many people cut chord bars for the key of E. Blank bars are available for the manufacturer. Another useful chord bar to cut would be the Dorian Mode. This imitates another banjo tuning known as Dorian or sawmill or mountain minor. The notes for this chord bar would be G, C, and D; similar to the ordinary G chord bar except the B has been changed to a C. Songs like Pretty Polly and Little Sadie and House Carpenter work well with this mode. The other chords used are F and occasionally Bb.

MOUNTAIN MUSIC PLAYED ON AUTOHARP - Folkways FA2365. Ernest Stoneman, Kilby Snow, Neriah & Kenneth Benfield, recorded by Mike Seeger. Collection of various country styles. Very good. Very important.

A SONG FOR YOU AND ME - Prestige 13058. Peggy Seeger. Use of 'harp on Death of Queen Jane (Child 170) and Peggy Gordon is excellent example of rhythmic complexity that can be achieved.

MOTHER MAYBELLE CARTER AND HER AUTOHARP - Smash MGS-27025. Autoharp solos with a "Nashville sound." Includes Bully of the Town, etc. Excellent.

ORIGINAL AND GREAT CARTER FAMILY - RCA Camden CAL586 ($1.98). Autoharp used as accompaniment, but many songs are adaptable as 'harp solos. Wildwood Flower, Lonesome Valley, Keep on the Sunny Side, etc. Similar to above.

NEW LOST CITY RAMBLERS, Vol 4 - Folkways FA2399. Tom Paley, Mike Seeger, John Cohen. Carter's Blues is the adaptation of a Carter tune to autoharp. Also includes Black Jack David.

SONGS OF THE CARTERS - Columbia CL1664. Maybelle Carter and Earl Scruggs playing autoharp and guitar, respectively. Very good.

Bibliography

OTHER BOOKS ON THE AUTOHARP

Cecil Null, "Pickin' Style for Autoharp," R. B. Fulgeson Music. 1963 "Many Ways to Play Autoharp" Vols. 1 & 2, Oscar Schmidt Intl. 1964.

BOOKS ON CARTER STYLE GUITAR

Harry A. Taussig, "Instrumental Techniques of American Folk Guitar," Traditional Stringed Instruments, 1964; Jerry Silverman,

"Folksingers Guitar Guide," Oak Publications 1963.

FINGERPICKING BOOKS FOR GUITAR THAT WILL HELP IN AUTOHARP PLAYING.

Harry A. Taussig, "Instrumental Techniques of American Folk Guitar," Traditional Stringed Instruments, 1964; Happy Traum, "Finger-Picking Styles for Guitar," Oak, 1966.

Some Other Publications of Interest From

OAK PUBLICATIONS
publishers & distributors of outstanding folk music books

1

2

3

4

5

Instruction Manuals

1) **The Art of The Folk-Blues Guitar/**
Jerry Silverman
The first instruction manual on folk-blues guitar method. Presents the styles of Josh White, Leadbelly, Big Bill Broonzy, and others. Tablature, Blues Arpeggio, Instrumental Breaks, Walking Bass and Boogie Woogie, Blues Strums plus many songs complete with words, music, chords and tablature. (both Meltab and Gitab)
$2.95/Illustrated

2) **Beginning The Folk Guitar/**
Jerry Silverman
A simplified detailed course in the first stages of playing the folk guitar, covering basic keys, runs, arpeggios, barre, use of capo, minor keys, etc. Illustrated with a chord chart and over 50 song examples.
$2.95/Illustrated

3) **Blues Harp/**
Tony "Little Sun" Glover
A full length presentation of blues harmonica playing based on the music of such great performers as Sonny Boy Williamson, Little Walter, Jimmy Reed and Sonny Terry.
$2.95/Illustrated

4) **The Chord-Player's Encyclopedia/**
Jerry Silverman
4700 chord diagrams, showing fingering and frets, for guitar (standard tuning, G Tuning, D Tuning, 12-String, Tenor), 5-String Banjo (G Tuning, C Tuning, D Tuning, G minor Tuning, Modal Tuning), Mandolin, Ukulele, Baritone Uke, Tenor Banjo, Piano, Organ, Accordion.
$2.95/Diagrams

5) **Country Blues Guitar/***Stefan Grossman*
An Instruction method and repertoire book based on the playing styles of foremost country blues guitarists. Includes guitar music, tablature, photographs for chord positions and strums, lyrics to songs, biographical background on Mississippi John Hurt, Blind Lemon, Son House, Mance Lipscomb, Charley Patton, Skip James, many others.
$2.95/Illustrated

6) **The Dulcimer Book** /*Jean Ritchie*
A manual for playing the Appalachian Dulcimer, with 16 illustrative songs, history of the instrument, etc.
$2.95/Illustrated

7) **Finger-Picking Styles For Guitar/**
Happy Traum
Documents and teaches the individual styles of the major influences in American guitar picking, including note-for-note transcriptions.
$2.95/Illustrated

8) **The Flat-Picker's Guitar Guide/**
Jerry Silverman
An instruction manual. A comprehensive analysis of the many different flat-picking techniques and styles. Includes over 40 songs arranged specifically for flat-picking and illustrated with "how to" drawings and diagrams.
$2.95/Illustrated

9) **The Folksinger's Guitar Guide/**
Jerry Silverman / Based on the Pete Seeger Recording
All music prepared on scales and in tablature. Includes sections on tuning, chord diagrams and chords, strums, transposing, use of barre and capo, etc. Plus over 30 songs complete with words, music, chords and tablature.
$2.95/Illustrated

10) **The Folksinger's Guitar Guide,**
Vol. 2/*Jerry Silverman*
The sequel to the country's number one folk guitar instruction book. For the intermediate and advanced guitar picker. Instruction and selection of songs. Music notations and guitar tablature.
$2.95/Illustrated

11) **A Folksinger's Guide To The 12-String Guitar As Played by Leadbelly/**
Julius Lester and Pete Seeger
The first instruction manual ever published for this increasingly popular instrument. Detailed instructions, folk song examples, tablature.
$2.95/Illustrated

12) **Folk Style Autoharp/***Harry Taussig*
An instruction method for playing the autoharp and accompanying folksongs. Beginning accompaniments, reading melodies, melody picking on autoharp, chords and keys, off-beats and syncopations, instrumental solos, etc. including 38 songs.
$2.95/Illustrated

13) **How To Play The Five-String Banjo/**
Pete Seeger
The basic manual for banjo players. Revised enlarged edition.
$2.00/Illustrated

14) **Note-Reading and Music Theory For Folk Guitarists/***Jerry Silverman*
An instruction manual that teaches the "stuff" of music to the folk guitarist in terms of folk songs instead of the traditional scales and abstract exercises.
$2.95/Illustrated

15) **The Recorder Guide/***Arthur Nitka and Johanna E. Kulbach*
The most complete guide to Soprano and Alto recorder playing by two experienced recorder teachers; combines basic progressive instruction with a great repertoire of folk melodies from many countries. Board covers, spiral binding.
$4.95/Illustrated

OAK PUBLICATIONS   33 West 60th Street   New York, N.Y. 10023